You are loved!

John Paul II to Aristotle
and Back Again

John Paul II to Aristotle
and Back Again

A Christian Philosophy of Life

ANDREW DEAN SWAFFORD

WIPF *&* STOCK · Eugene, Oregon

JOHN PAUL II TO ARISTOTLE AND BACK AGAIN
A Christian Philosophy of Life

Wipf & Stock
An Imprint of Wipf and Stock Publishers
199 W. 8th Ave., Suite 3
Eugene, OR 97401

www.wipfandstock.com

ISBN 13: 978-1-4982-0354-8

Manufactured in the U.S.A.

I dedicate this work to my wife and three children (and our fourth child who is on the way!).

I also dedicate this work in a special way to Dr. Edward Sri, my first teacher in the school of virtue.

Contents

Acknowledgments

I WOULD LIKE TO thank David Trotter, director of Campus Ministry at Benedictine College, for inviting me to give a talk on John Paul II during the week of his canonization in the spring of 2014. My paper was originally entitled, "John Paul II to Aristotle and Back Again: A Disciple's Tale." This book developed from that paper.

I would also like to thank the students of Benedictine College where I currently teach in the Theology Department. They are a delight to teach, and their enthusiasm for learning and insightful questions over the years have surely sharpened this book.

Thanks also to my wife who has just published *Emotional Virtue: A Guide to Drama-Free Relationships*; supporting each other through these projects has been a wonderful experience. And thanks also to my children for their patience throughout this process.

I would also like to thank Wipf and Stock; they have been absolutely terrific to work with, both on the publication of my earlier volume, *Nature and Grace: A New Approach to Thomistic Ressourcement*, as well as on this project.

Last but certainly not least, I would like to thank my very dear friend, Fr. Cajetan Cuddy, OP, both for the great blessing of his friendship, as well as his thorough reading of the entire manuscript. His feedback has certainly improved this work. But of course, I am alone responsible for any infelicities that still remain in the text.

And thanks most of all to Almighty God, in whom "we live and move and have our being" (Acts 17:28). I remain in awe of his providence.

Introduction

THIS BOOK AIMS TO set forth a concise moral and philosophical vision of reality which is rooted in Aristotle and which flowers well beyond the Greek philosopher in the thought of St. John Paul II. At least one person who appears in the text as a medium between the two is St. Thomas Aquinas, though not so much for his own sake, but more as a Christian interpreter of this basic philosophical framework.

While this book is not a manual on Christian or Catholic apologetics, it does address the following: God's existence and his relationship to the natural order; the interplay of faith and reason; a classical understanding of human nature and the life of virtue which springs from it; as well as John Paul II's analysis of the "language" of the body and the meaning of human love and sexuality.

While this is an unabashedly Christian and Catholic book, the accent mark has been placed here on its being *philosophical*. That is, this book aims to provide the philosophical underpinnings for a Christian and Catholic worldview—and while it does so from within the context of faith, this book seeks to lay out these philosophical foundations in a way that is accessible (at least, in principle) to someone who does not share Christian or Catholic faith; whether the non-believer finds them convincing is of course another question altogether. Thus, this work aims to elucidate the particular philosophical principles involved and the connection between the principles and the conclusions drawn, much more so than simply being an apologetic attempt aimed at convincing non-believers. In other words, the goal here is more to cultivate a deep *understanding* than simple persuasion.

But insofar as dialogue is advanced by mutual understanding, I do believe this text will further the cause of evangelization. It will also bear out—as is my conviction—that our disagreements with those not sharing our faith are very much fundamental and philosophical in nature. For this reason, the most superficially persuasive argument may not be the one that does the most good in the end; whereas, a deep understanding of the issues involved may cultivate more respect from the opposing side, regardless of whether or not they are persuaded to change their minds. Consequently, for my part, cultivating a greater respect for, and fostering a deeper understanding of, our worldview, at its most fundamental levels, will bring about greater fruit in the long run.

This is very much the case because what is at issue is much like what Thomas Kuhn described in the history of science as particular "paradigms" at work.[1] Kuhn's point was that what actually happened in various scientific revolutions throughout history (he focuses entirely on physics and chemistry) has more to do with "paradigm shifts" than the simple accumulation of new data; that is, for his part, a scientific revolution occurs when data is looked at from a different vantage point, and the new theory has more explanatory power and fewer "anomalies," in his words.[2] Put in philosophical terms, the point is this: often reasoning occurs *within* a particular paradigm, from which a rational defense of one's position can be mustered; but disagreements often are the result of *different paradigms*—wherein each side is able to marshal a rational defense, but with the appearance of a stalemate between two incommensurable paradigms. The reason is that it's difficult to adjudicate which paradigm is right—but the point is that each side's "case" makes sense within (and only within) their own particular paradigm.

---

1. Kuhn, *Structure of Scientific Revolutions.* See also his, *Copernican Revolution: Planetary Astronomy in the Development of Western Thought.*

2. See Kuhn, *Structure of Scientific Revolutions,* 52–65.

What this means for Christian apologetics and the proclamation of the Gospel is this: perhaps we ought to spend more time *explaining* our paradigm than simply engaging in arguments aimed at persuasion; for the simple truth is that unless someone changes paradigms, they may well never "see" the truth that we see. Thus, this book aims to unpack the deeper foundations of a Christian and Catholic philosophical paradigm. It offers reasons that can be understood by all; but admittedly, the philosophical reflection and reasoning undertaken in the following has been nurtured and fostered from within a tradition of faith. That said, again, it is largely philosophical, utilizing premises and principles accessible to believer and non-believer alike.

Let us now turn to set the stage for what is to follow, pointing to the twin pillars of our exposition, Aristotle and St. John Paul II.

In light of the recent canonization of St. John Paul II in the spring of 2014, I'd like to propose him as a model for Christian intellectuals, one who unites head and heart—at one and the same time, contemplative and evangelist. I wish particularly to show how an understanding of the natural order rooted in Aristotle and the life of virtue which springs from it helps to inform then-Karol Wojtyla's thought in his 1960-work *Love and Responsibility*, which later blossomed into the *Theology of the Body*. I'd also like to suggest that what's happening in *Love and Responsibility* is a good example of "*Christian* Philosophy," as understood and sanctioned by Pope John Paul II.

In what follows, we will move in three distinct phases: first (chapters 1 and 2), we begin with the issue of God's existence and his relation to the natural order; then we will turn to a treatment of faith and reason, with an eye toward elucidating the issues surrounding Christian philosophy.

Second (chapters 3, 4, and 5), in terms of exploring what reason can do, we will survey the Aristotelian foundations of virtue, and their relation to human nature and human happiness, noting how the Christian tradition has absorbed and enhanced this virtue framework.

Third (chapters 7 and 8), we will turn to Wojtyla's *Love and Responsibility*,[3] in order to see how he absorbs—and goes beyond—the Aristotelian framework of virtue in order to create, as he puts it, a synthesis between the "personal order" and the "natural order." Here, we will build upon earlier material and explore his exposition of the nuptial meaning of the body and human love, a nuptial meaning which expresses the human vocation to make of one's life a total gift of self.

We now turn to the issue of God's existence and his relation to the natural order.

---

3. Sometimes when referring to John Paul II's work before he became pope I will refer to him by his birth name, Karol Wojtyla; other times I will refer to him simply as John Paul II, even when the reference is to an earlier work before his pontificate. Also, the reader may have noticed that I skipped chapter 6 in my brief summary. In that chapter, I will tell my personal story about how I went from playing small college football to embracing Jesus Christ. Many of the ideas throughout this book were pivotal in my transformation.

1

God and the Natural Order

FOR THE CHRISTIAN, FAITH and reason are two ways of know-ing, two ways of accessing different dimensions of reality—"two wings" upon which the human spirit soars to truth, in John Paul II's memorable expression.[1] For some thinkers, faith and reason are seen as unfriendly partners in dialogue—if one is up, the other is down, and vice versa. But this is not the case for the classical Catholic synthesis, a synthesis which sees a true marriage estab-lished in God's providence between "Jerusalem" and "Athens," between faith and reason. In the classical Catholic synthesis, the higher "nature" goes (the realm of natural reason, our human pur-suit of the natural good), the higher "grace" soars (i.e., the realm accessible only by faith and by divine initiative and disclosure).[2]

1. Pope John Paul II, *Fides et Ratio*. This quote occurs at the outset, before the main body of the document.

2. When I speak of the orders of nature and grace, "nature" here means both the natural order of the universe and "human nature," in particular, sometimes with a primary focus on the latter. As will be seen more clearly later, the order of nature does *not* mean a realm where God's influence is absent. God is the cause and sustainer of both the orders of nature and of grace; the difference is that in the order of grace God raises man above what would be possible for him by the principles inherent in human nature alone. As an analogy, a stained-glass window has its own perfection and beauty; but a

Indeed, the cathedrals of faith are not built on the sands of a tepid and timid reason, but just the opposite. The boldness of faith and the boldness of reason stand together.[3]

THE NATURAL ORDER
AS THE EMBODIMENT OF DIVINE WISDOM

This confidence in natural reason and this appreciation for the beauty and goodness of the natural order stems from the conviction that God is the author of both the orders of nature and of grace. In a real sense, the order of nature is *the embodiment of divine wisdom*. For this reason, the scientist who studies the laws of nature can be seen as quite literally *retracing God's thoughts after him*: the reason is because the order of nature first existed in the Mind of the Creator, and was thence "thought" into existence— much as an architect first draws up a blueprint for a building in his mind, and perhaps on paper, which is only later embodied in brick and mortar.[4] When the building is constructed, one can rightly view the building as the embodiment of an idea—the embodiment of what first existed in the architect's mind. Likewise, the created order of nature is the embodiment of an idea that first existed in the divine mind,[5] a view expressed here in the *Catechism of the Catholic Church* this way: "The things of the world and the things of faith derive from the same God. The humble and persevering investigator of the secrets of nature is being led, as it were, by the

---

stained-glass window illumined by the sun is even more radiant and beautiful still. The stained-glass window by itself is like the perfection of human nature, animated by its own natural principles; the stained-glass window illumined by the sun is like human nature transformed and elevated by grace. For this analogy and its principles developed further, see my *Nature and Grace*, 88–100.

3. See John Paul II: "The *parrhesia* [Greek for "boldness"] of faith must be matched by the boldness of reason" (*Fides et Ratio*, 48).

4. This is the Eternal Law, for Aquinas, the "Divine Reason's conception of things." *ST* I–IIae, q. 91, a. 1. See also *ST* I–IIae, q. 93, a. 1. This reference is to St. Thomas Aquinas' *Summa Theologiae* and will be cited this way throughout.

5. Cf. *ST* I, q. 15, a. 2.

hand of God in spite of himself, for it is God, the conserver of all things, who made them what they are."[6]

This, of course, does not in any way imply that the scientist must be consciously aware of the divine origin of the order of nature in order to do science; but it is to say that from the context of creation (and belief in a Creator), the natural order represents at one level the wisdom and providence of the Creator, resulting in a *greater* (not lesser) Christian appreciation for the order of nature. Too often, Christians see God's wisdom and will at work *only* in the supernatural, a perspective occasionally at work in discussions regarding Intelligent Design and evolution—since such a dichotomy appears to suggest that what is caused by nature *cannot* also be caused by God, that the two are in a zero-sum game of competition in which one is the winner and the other necessarily the loser. Such a competitive view of God and nature is absolutely not the classical Catholic philosophical conception.[7]

In contrast, the perspective advocated here does not in any way neglect the supernatural, but insists on the relevance of the order of nature—an order which does in fact express the wisdom of divine providence. In other words, we can say that, *ordinarily*, God

---

6. *Catechism of the Catholic Church*, 159. Here after, abbreviated as CCC.

7. See Schönborn, *Chance or Purpose*, 43: "We believe in a Creator who is not just one cause among others, intervening from time to time, when things get too difficult or when you reach some limit." Related is this comment from Brad Gregory, in his analysis of the shift from the classical Catholic philosophical conception to the more modern (competitive) view of God's relation to nature: "It is self-evident that a God who by definition is radically distinct from the natural world could never be shown to be unreal via empirical inquiry that by definition can only investigate the natural world. To posit some link between science and the unreality of God therefore presupposes that God is in some sense being conceived as part of the universe—or, in Christian categories, that God and creation have been in some way combined, conflated, or confused . . . . Similarly, to think that science has falsified or could falsify claims about God's presence in and through the natural world presupposes that scientific explanations about causality in the universe exclude any possible simultaneous or supervening divine presence. That is, it assumes that natural and supernatural causality . . . comprise a zero-sum game, a sort of competitive, either-or relationship between God and creation." Gregory, *The Unintended Reformation*, 32.

works through the medium of the natural order; sometimes, he works directly—we call those occasions "miracles."[8] But the point to stress is this: when "nature" does something, this does not mean that God is uninvolved. As Creator, God gives to creation the gift of existence and is the cause of its most fundamental order; his causality at this most basic level means that he does not *compete* with the natural order, but rather he gives nature its ability to be a cause at all in the first place.

As an analogy, which bears the fruit—the tree or the branch? Well, both—the tree gives the branch its ability to bear the fruit in the first place; the branch does something real, but it is in a deeper way dependent upon the tree. In a similar way, God is radically other than the universe; he is not a great big creature in competition with other creatures; rather, God is the cause of the very *being* (or *existence*) of creatures at their most fundamental level—he causes their being and gives them their distinctive nature, giving them the capacity to be what they are and do what they do, as real causes, and expressing in their own unique way a glimpse of divine wisdom, and even showing forth some perfection which pre-exists in the Creator. Metaphysically, not only is creation good, but each and every aspect of creation exhibits some intelligible reality— some perfection—that pre-exists in God.[9]

---

8. See Schönborn, *Chance or Purpose*, 43.

9. See *ST* I, q. 13, a. 3. See Schönborn: "Every creature, whether it be a star or a stone, a plant or a tree, an animal or a human being, reflects the perfection and the goodness of God in its own particular fashion" (Schönborn, *Chance or Purpose*, 60). For this reason, creation does not *add* anything to God's glory; rather, creation *expresses* and *manifests* God's glory. And it's extremely fitting that we have such a plethora and variety of creatures; for how else can finite beings express the Infinite? In other words, perfections which are unified in the One and Infinite God—when they are embodied in finite creatures—must be manifested in a polyvalent variety, since no one creature could express the perfections of the Infinite Creator. To use an analogy, what is unified in white light—when it strikes a prism—is manifested in all the colors of the rainbow. Similarly, perfections which pre-exist in the One and Infinite God are fittingly made manifest in finite beings precisely through their manifold diversity.

GOD AND THE FOUNDATIONS OF SCIENCE

In fact, it was this Christian metaphysical vision of reality that helped pave the way for the rise of modern science—which was birthed in the heart of late medieval Christian culture.[10] Consider some of the following Christian presuppositions that greatly abetted the rise of science: (1) belief in a *rational creator*, which naturally leads to the assumption of a stable and predictable order of nature, with its own proper and discoverable laws; (2) belief that *creation is good* (if matter and creation were considered intrinsically evil, then one would not be likely to show much interest in science);[11] (3) belief in the radical *distinction between the creature and the Creator*—that is, no pantheism (if one believed that creation were "divine," or that random "gods" were controlling various aspects of the phenomena of nature, then one likely would not be inclined to pursue what we know as science); and (4) belief that *our minds can understand something about the created order*; in light of the belief that we are made in the "image and likeness of God" (Gen 1:26), this conviction makes good sense.[12]

As to third point, in a real way, biblical Christian faith "demythologizes" the natural order,[13] showing, for example, the sun to be a mere "creature" and not a deity; the Christian view of creation demystifies the created order, showing that much of natural phenomena is just that—*natural* phenomena, and not the realm of multifarious and competing gods.

10. See Jaki, *Savior of Science*. See also Woods, *How the Catholic Church Built Western Civilization*, 67–114. See especially Hannam, *God's Philosophers*.

11. The goodness of creation is asserted as a fundamental tenet of biblical faith in Gen 1, a view which is dramatically on display in the doctrine of the Incarnation, as well as the sacraments—God using matter and flesh to bring about our salvation. It was generally gnostic Christianity—not orthodox Christianity—that held to an extremely low of view of matter and the body.

12. See Rizzi, *The Science Before Science*, 187.

13. See Schönborn, *Chance or Purpose*, 20: "The Bible is the first agent of enlightenment. In a certain sense, it 'disenchants' the world; it divests it of its magical and mythical power, 'demythologizes' the world, and 'banishes the gods.'"

Some of these ideas lie behind what has come to be known as the "Regensburg Address" by Pope Emeritus Benedict, given in September of 2006.[14] In that lecture, Benedict suggested that *the very practice of science raises a question that goes beyond science*; what he meant was that the very practice of science assumes what theologians and philosophers refer to as the "intelligibility" of the natural order; that is, the "understandability" of the universe. In other words, for science to operate, one has to assume a real order embedded in the universe, which can then be investigated and discovered and understood further by the practice of science.[15] Even if we don't know the cause of some phenomena, we reasonably assume that some rational causal explanation exists in principle, and that's why we make our investigation into nature in the first place, in order to uncover what that explanation is. But if we had assumed that nature were chaotic and not rational, then we would never have bothered to search for rational causes at all in the first place.

The Emeritus Pope's point, then, is this: what makes sense of this tenacious assumption of the *orderliness* of the natural order which is so critical to all of science? Why should non-rational material entities function according to mathematical laws? Why are there laws of nature *at all* in the first place? Benedict's implicit point is that such an assumption of the intelligibility of nature makes a good bit of sense in light of our belief in a Creator; but it's left unexplained otherwise. In other words, the world is rational because the Divine Mind preceded the material universe; the universe is thus the embodiment of a divine idea, the embodiment of divine wisdom.

For this reason, St. Thomas Aquinas can say that all created reality stands, as it were, between "two minds"—between the Divine Mind who created it and our finite minds who can understand it.[16] The word "recognize" can be understood to give implicit

14. See Schall, *The Regensburg Lecture*.

15. See Barr, *Modern Physics and Ancient Faith*, 76-92.

16. See Schönborn, *Chance or Purpose*, 139; the citation from Aquinas is found in *de Veritate* I, 2.

witness to this point, as when we "recognize" the order of the universe; for the word can be broken down into "re-cognize" (i.e., a "re-knowing"): thus, when we study the order of the universe, we *re*-cognize it—we come to know what was first known in the mind of the Creator beforehand. There is always first an order already embedded within the universe, put there, according to the Christian understanding, because an Infinite Mind stands at the origin of all things, indeed prior to all things.

These same ideas stand behind the famous quote from Albert Einstein: "The fact that it [the world] is comprehensible is a miracle."[17] His point, again, is that the very intelligibility of the universe—its fundamental order which makes science even possible in the first place—is not something to be simply taken for granted, but is rather a truly astonishing fact. It should put us in a position of awe and wonder; and this wonder, on the Christian reading, implies that Mind came before matter, not the other way around; that is, the Divine Architect knew all things and "thinks" all things into existence in his act of creation.[18] As we have said, therefore, when we study the order of nature, we are in a strange and wonderful way retracing his thoughts after him. Let us close here with the words of one of the most famous atheists—now-turned-theist—of the twentieth century, Anthony Flew, who comments on this very issue as follows:

> If you accept the fact that there are laws, then something must impose that regularity on the universe . . . . Those scientists who point to the Mind of God do not merely advance a series of arguments or a process of syllogistic reasoning. Rather, they propound a vision of reality that emerges from the conceptual heart of modern science

---

17. As cited in *Ideas and Opinions by Albert Einstein*, trans., Sonja Bargmann, 292. See also Flew, *There is a God*, 101–02.

18. See Ratzinger, *Introduction to Christianity*, trans. J. R. Foster, 106–08. "This surely means that all our thinking is indeed only a re-thinking of what in reality has already been thought out beforehand" (ibid., 106). This text was originally published in German as *Einführung in das Christentum*, 1968.

and imposes itself on the rational mind. It is a vision that
I personally find compelling and irrefutable.[19]

GOD AS CAUSE OF EXISTENCE

Here we will continue our reflection with a focus on the notions of
contingency and necessity.[20] Right here, in fact, is where the theist
and the non-theist part ways: if the universe is contingent, it does
not explain itself and therefore points beyond itself to the Creator;
on the other hand, if the universe does explain itself, then it is
"necessary" and needs no further explanation beyond itself. For
the theist, it makes sense to ask *why is there something rather than
nothing—why does anything exist at all?* And likewise, it makes
sense to ask *why is the universe ordered at all in the first place, and
why does it have the particular order it does* (not just with respect
to this or that organism, but the basic order expressed in the most
fundamental laws of physics).

The reason these questions make sense is because at the end
of the day the universe's existence and its most fundamental order
are *contingent* facts, not *necessary* truths. We can see this more
clearly by a comparison with necessary truths. Necessary truths
are truths which could not be other than they are. For example,
that "5" is a prime number is necessarily true—given the nature of
"5" and the definition of what it means to be prime, it could not be
otherwise; "5" *must* be a prime number.

On the other hand, the truth that "there is a tree in my front
yard" is contingent, precisely because—while true—it could certainly have been otherwise. Even though there is truly a tree in
my front yard, many possible causal scenarios could be construed
wherein there would be no tree in my yard (or perhaps a different

19. Flew, *There is a God*, 110, 112.

20. As we will see, "contingency" basically refers to dependency; that is,
if a thing is contingent, it is dependent upon other things. Conversely, if a
thing is necessary, its existence is *not* dependent upon other things. Key to
the discussion here is that what is contingent demands a causal explanation
outside of itself.

tree). Because there are many causal factors that contributed to there being a tree in my front yard, it makes perfect sense to ask "why" or "how" that tree got there, or "why" it is the particular way it is. Conversely, it doesn't make much sense to ask "why" of a necessary truth; it doesn't make sense to ask why "5" is a prime number—it just *is*, by definition, and could not have been otherwise.[21]

So the question before us is this: is the existence of the universe and the fact that it exhibits a deep and underlying order (which makes science possible) a *necessary* or *contingent* fact? In other words, is the universe's existence more like "5" being prime, or is it more like the fact that there is a tree in my front yard? If the universe were necessary in the strict sense, it could not be otherwise than it is; and if it were necessary, it wouldn't make any sense to ask "why" it is the way it is or how it got to be here in the first place. But the great metaphysical question—*why is there something rather than nothing*—is a real question, one which makes sense to ask, despite its difficulty to answer. Further, Big Bang cosmology certainly negates a static universe that simply always was and is.[22] Thus, the universe appears to be contingent—and a contingent being never fully explains itself, but rather points beyond itself to its ultimate explanation.[23]

Philosophical reflection points in the same direction. For the philosophical tradition going back to the likes of Plato, the following are clear marks of contingency: that which changes, is material or physical, could be other than it is, and does not fully account for itself. Conversely, signs that a thing is *necessary* in the strict sense are: that it cannot change, it is immaterial, could not be otherwise than it is, and it fully accounts for itself. As we suggested with the example of "5" being a prime number, mathematical truths give the closest approximation to necessity, precisely

21. See Barr, *Modern Physics and Ancient Faith*, 263–65.

22. See Spitzer, *New Proofs for the Existence of God*, 24–8. Also, Barr, *Modern Physics and Ancient Faith*, 47–61.

23. See Adler, *How to Think about God*, 144: "Whatever can be otherwise than it is can also simply not be at all . . . . A merely possible cosmos [i.e., a contingent universe] cannot be an uncaused cosmos . . . . [It] needs a supernatural cause."

because mathematics transcends the changing material order. In other words, for example, two plus two equals four—regardless of whether we're talking about two cows, two dogs, or two flowers; and even if the universe ceased to exist, this mathematical truth would still be true.

Thus, as soon as we know that something is physical, changeable, could be otherwise than it is, and does not fully account for itself, we know that it is ultimately contingent. And that which is contingent reduces back to something that is necessary; for to posit an everlasting contingent entity, with no explanation for its existence beyond itself, is simply to leave things unexplained.

In order to show that contingency always points to something beyond itself that is necessary, let us use the analogy of a chain hanging in the sky. Suppose someone asked me why the chain was hanging there and I simply answered, "Well, there are an infinite number of chain links going upward." This explanation would not be adequate because it would not explain why the chain is hanging in the sky in the first place. But on the other hand, suppose I pointed out that the chain is hanging from a tree or skyscraper—now I would be starting to get somewhere. The reason is because, in the analogy, the tree or the skyscraper "explain their own upright standing," and in a certain sense account for themselves. So, in the analogy, that which does not explain itself (the chain hanging in the sky) must reduce back to something that does explain itself (the tree or the skyscraper).[24]

Similarly, to give another analogy: suppose someone asked me why a series of train cars were moving, and I simply responded that there were an infinite number of cars—and I further noted that *none of them had an engine*—would I have explained the motion of the train? No, because the movement of each train car (with no engine) is contingent—that is to say dependent—upon its being pulled by the car in front of it. The motion of the cars (whose motion is *dependent* [i.e., contingent]) must be explained ultimately by a car whose motion is *independent*—that is, a car that

24. See Rizzi, *The Science Before Science*, 266.

can account for its own motion.[25] In these analogies, accordingly, God is represented by the tree (or skyscraper) and the train car with an engine, and the chain hanging in the sky or the train cars with no engine represent all of creation.

In the Christian tradition, only God is necessary in the strict and absolute sense. Even the highest of the angels don't explain their own existence. To use the language of the Thomistic tradition, there is a distinction in every creature between *what* it is (its essence or nature) and the fact that it is (its existence). Only in God are essence and existence one, such that God could *not* not exist—which is to say that God is necessary in the strict and absolute sense; everything else, in which there is a distinction between essence and existence, is contingent.[26]

Reflecting upon the intelligible orderliness of the natural order and its ultimate contingency shows the *reasonableness* of faith beyond what can be seen and touched; the changing material universe cannot have the last word; indeed, the presence of rationality *in* the universe (its order and intelligibility) implies a Rationality *beyond* the universe. This is the Christian conception

25. See *ST* I, q. 2, a. 3. It's this type of series of dependent or contingent movers that Aquinas denies can have an infinite regress: "subsequent movers move only inasmuch as they are put in motion by the first mover; *as the staff moves only because it is put in motion by the hand*" (emphasis added).

26. See *ST* I, q. 3, a. 3 and 4. Similarly is Aquinas' use of the language of "participation," which basically refers to something possessing some attribute *contingently*, as in the following example of iron becoming hot by fire (notice, iron does not account for its own heat—its heat is contingent on something that has heat of itself, e.g., fire). Aquinas writes: "For whatever is found in anything by participation, must be caused in it by that to which it belongs essentially, as iron becomes ignited by fire" (*ST* I, q. 44, a. 1). St. Thomas carries this analogy forward to describe existence—God has existence of himself; all other creatures participate in existence: "God is the essentially self-subsisting Being . . . . Therefore all beings apart from God are not their own being [i.e., they are contingent], but are beings by participation. Therefore it must be that all things which are diversified by the diverse participation of being, so as to be more or less perfect, are caused by the one First Being, Who possesses being most perfectly" (ibid.). Similarly, he writes: "from the fact that a thing has being by participation [i.e., does not fully explain itself], it follows that it is caused" (ibid., ad 1). See Barron, *The Priority of Christ*, 228–29 and *Bridging the Great Divide*, 135.

of the Creator, one who is radically other than the universe, but yet paradoxically one who is also astonishingly immanent in that he is the cause of our very being (existence) and our nature (or essence). That is, he causes us and holds us in being at our most fundamental core, giving creatures the gift of existence and their particular nature which allows them to be what they are and do what they do.[27] God has his existence of himself; all other creatures participate in the gift of existence—a gift of which God is the ultimate and constant source.[28]

GOD AND HUMAN NATURE

Practically, as far as man is concerned, the above discussion means we should not look to God's action upon us in the manner of a pool table—as if we were billiard balls set in motion by the divine cue ball. God works through all things in accordance with and through their nature (after all, he is cause of that nature);[29] for us, that means he works through us as *rational* and *free* agents. This means that, for example, our inexorable desire for happiness— something that is inbuilt into our nature and which propels us in life to make choices in search of fulfilling this infinite desire—is the primordial way by which God moves us, drawing us back to himself, whether we realize it or not.[30] If we reflect upon it, we realize that we don't really *choose* whether or not we want to be happy; after all, if we decided we didn't want to be happy, we must think we would be happier that way! Rather, our desire for happiness is not something chosen, but is prerequisite (and prior) to all of our free choices; indeed, as we said, our desire for happiness is the

27. See *ST* I, q. 105, a. 5: "Because in all things God is properly the cause of universal being, which is innermost in all things, it follows that in all things God works intimately."

28. See note 26 above.

29. See *ST* I–IIae, q. 91, a. 2: "it is evident that all things partake somewhat of the eternal law, in so far as, namely, from its being imprinted on them, they derive their respective inclinations to their proper acts and ends."

30. See *ST* I, q. 2, a. 2, ad 1.

Creator's initial way of ordering us on our journey, a journey that ultimately has its destination in himself.

In this light, he orders us and moves us—not in spite of ourselves—but through our very selves. This shows us at one level that the divine movement in our souls is not incompatible with human freedom: for at the natural level, God orders us to the true and the good by planting within us an inclination toward infinite happiness, an inclination that is prior to all our choices. This desire for happiness moves us to freely seek the true and the good in the finite things around us. In this way, God draws us back to himself, yet through our own voluntary action.

The happiness we desire is infinite and yet even the greatest goods of this life are finite. Part of the journey, then, is coming to see that this infinite desire for happiness is a sign that—as great as this life is—we are made for something even greater still.

CONCLUSION

Here we have laid the foundations for the reasonableness of our faith in a Creator and have seen God's relation to the created natural order: the latter is the embodiment of divine wisdom. Moreover, God is not a competitive cause with the natural order; rather, he is the cause of the existence and nature of things. Thus, his causality is actually prerequisite to nature's ability to be a cause at all. In this light, the relationship between God and the natural order is decidedly *non*-competitive. We also have explored briefly what this means for understanding God's relation to human nature and God's moving of us *through* our most fundamental desire for happiness—a desire which moves us back to himself, whether we are conscious of this or not.

But of course this is not the end of our discussion; rather, Christian faith is all about a God in search of man—a God who became one of us in Jesus Christ.[31] The trick, then, in this Christian and Catholic synthesis of faith and reason is striking a balance

31. See Lewis, *Miracles*, 187.

between, on the one hand, recognizing distinguishable realities (faith and reason, an order of grace and an order of nature), but without, on the other hand, seeming to imply two separate universes, as it were—one of nature and one of grace. There is *one* universe, which is permeated by God's providence in different ways, at different levels.

It is in the context of this Catholic synthesis of faith and reason—as distinguishable, but ultimately ordered toward union with one another—that we will engage below the prospects and legitimacy of "Christian philosophy." Paradoxically, it is perhaps true that Christian philosophical reason excels most when it is accompanied by the light of faith. And so we now turn to the issues surrounding Christian philosophy, first looking at objections against it, and then offering reasons in its favor; we will conclude with John Paul II's view of the matter, pointing to him as a model for us in the twenty-first century.

2

Faith, Reason,
and Christian Philosophy

THE CASE AGAINST

THE ISSUE OF CHRISTIAN philosophy was a disputed one among Thomists in the early part of the twentieth century and for good reason,[1] as a proper balance needed to be struck. Those opposed to the notion of *Christian* philosophy pointed out that we don't have *"Christian* Chemistry" or *"Christian* math," so what's behind the appellation of *"Christian"* philosophy? Is it ultimately due to a lack of confidence in reason's ability to do philosophy—is that then why the appellation "Christian" must be brought into play in order to rescue reason's operation?

Indeed, there is a danger here that a certain type of *fideism* and *scientism* are often more closely aligned than we might at first realize. For our purposes, "scientism" simply refers to the view concerning the nature and limits of knowledge that confines our

1. See Veatch, "The Problems and the Prospects of a Christian Philosophy—Then and Now," *The Monist* 75 (1992): 381–91 and Nédoncelle, *Is There a Christian Philosophy?*, trans. Illtyd Trethowan.

knowing to what can be verified through the scientific method. Put aside for now whether *metaphysical* theories about the nature and limits of knowledge can be verified by this same scientific method![2] By "fideism," I am referring to a position that holds that any attempt at answering the important human questions (e.g., God's existence, basic morality) can only come by way of faith, not reason. Hence, let us take note of the fact that fideism and scientism are often flipsides of the very same coin along the following lines: *all things we can really know by natural reason, we know by science; those things that go beyond science, we can only know by faith.* What gets lost in the shuffle, then, are what the Catholic tradition calls the *praeambula fidei* or, the "preambles to faith"—things like God's existence, the soul, the nature of the human person, basic morality, natural law and the like. These things are revealed or implied in Revelation, but they are also in principle accessible to reason—unlike, say, the Blessed Trinity which can only be known by faith and God's revealing of his own inner life to us.

What we have here is what our Emeritus Pope Benedict referred to in his Regensburg Address as the *reduction in the radius of reason*;[3] if reason can only deal with those things which can be quantified and measured, then everything else gets relegated to faith, especially those things which are most essential and precious to human existence. But these most important things then get marginalized as merely subjective and private expressions of faith; that is, they are no longer something available for the public discourse of reason. And so God is removed from our schools and separation of church and State goes from being an anti-establishment clause (i.e., the U.S. won't be like the Church of England with an officially established and state-sponsored religion), to a scenario where the State must quash any "religious" expression whatsoever.[4] Conse-

2. In other words, "scientism" is a *philosophical* position regarding the nature and limits of knowledge, not a scientific one, subject to empirical verification and falsification.

3. See Schall, *The Regensburg Lecture.*

4. See Chaput, *Render unto Caesar*, 86: "The First Amendment's religion clause merely states that 'Congress shall make no law respecting an establishment of religion, or prohibiting the free exercise thereof'. Scholars differ

quently, what was once the robust realm of natural reason is now a private judgment, a subjective and merely "religious" claim; these examples are on full display when the pro-life position is relegated in such a manner.[5]

Thus, the more the purview of reason is restricted, the more any claim beyond that purview is publically marginalized. And though it may sound "pious" and modest to relegate all knowledge of such important matters to the realm of faith, we are actually marginalizing ourselves in the process.

---

sharply on what the clause really mandates. For 'strict separationists', it means that government should be religion-neutral, even to the point of state hostility to any official public recognition of religion. For 'nonpreferentialists', it means that government is free to acknowledge and even support religion, so long as no single religious group gets preferred treatment."

5. The pro-life position is based on the view that when the life of the new human organism begins, the person comes into existence. Interestingly, it's often the pro-choice side—at least in academic circles—that avoids the question as to when the human organism begins and focuses more on questions of "personhood," often opting to frame personhood (which is when they take moral and legal rights to begin) in terms of self-consciousness and awareness. But such of a view "personhood" is very slippery—after all, how "self-conscious" is a three-month old? What we want is to "divide nature at its joints," as it were, and to do so we need to look at the nature of things—how they act and react. A sperm left to itself will never become a mature human being. But a newly conceived embryo has everything it needs internally to self-develop into a mature human being. This radical difference in potency (or self-developing capacity) between a sperm and a newly conceived embryo is enough to note a radical difference in nature between the two. Therefore, the sperm is a *potential human being*—say, if it were to later join with an ovum; but an embryo is a *human being with potential*. In other words, the movement from sperm and ovum individually, to their joining in conception is a *substantial change*—a change in *kind*, whereby a new individual comes about. Whereas, the movement from embryo to fetus to birth to growth and maturation into adulthood—these are all *accidental changes*, that is, developments of one and the same individual that came into existence at conception. Notice that none of the claims I just made are inherently "religious" or wrapped up in questions of when the soul is infused or the like. My claims are not strictly "scientific" either, though there are points of contact. Rather, my claims here are all strictly *philosophical*, that is, accessible to public reason—but not a public reason which has *a priori* reduced itself to the quantifiable and the measurable. See Beckwith, *Defending Life*, 65–73.

Accordingly, those who were resistant to the notion of "Christian" philosophy worried about this very trajectory of abdicating a robust confidence in reason's ability to ask and answer the great human questions. They worried that though the appellation "Christian" as a modifier of philosophy sounded pious, this move seemed more due to a capitulation to modernity—that is, to a modern view of reason which tends to restrict what reason can do to the empirically verifiable and the measurable.

Something similar happened to theology: the more theology capitulated to modernity's restricted view of reason, the more theology had to remake itself into a primarily *historical* discipline. This new mode of thinking would produce a theology devoid of conviction—in a sense, a theology devoid of faith; it would no longer seek the truth *per se*, but instead would simply seek to offer neutral explanations regarding *who* said *what* and *when* and *why*. Theology, in this sense, becomes the history of religious opinions; and accordingly, it came to retitle itself "*Religious Studies*" on that very account.

THE CASE FOR

While the case against "Christian" philosophy was due to the perception that the restyling of philosophy as "Christian" was due to a dwindling confidence in reason in its classical sense, on the other hand, we do have to ask ourselves: do we sincerely believe that the faith is true? Because if we do, isn't it obviously the case that the faith helps us to reason more reasonably—to better see the truth and to suggest more fruitful lines of inquiry than would otherwise be the case? It would seem, then, that the believer must have a genuine place for Christian philosophy.

Consider the following example drawn from biblical studies: does a biblical exegete feel *enlightened* or *restricted* by ecclesiastical dogma? The modern answer readily tends toward the latter; but is this not greatly abetted and reinforced by a contemporary notion of freedom—freedom as *freedom of choice*, the *autonomy* to decide for oneself? If scholarship is purely about exploring *options*, then I suppose church dogma means that some options are off the table. But if scholarship, especially theological scholarship, is about apprehending and beholding the fullness of truth, then pure freedom of choice is not the end goal; the exploring of options and the defense of positions is not the summit of wisdom, as if the ability to play "intellectual ping pong" made one a genuine scholar. Rather, discerning the truth and joyfully embracing the truth is the mark of theological wisdom, an embrace which should lead to the transformation of mind and heart. In this sense, dogmas are like "lights on the road," illuminating the path and suggesting new avenues of research that are more likely to be fruitful than others.

Here's an analogy that came to me during my undergraduate days: in junior high and high school math texts, what do we typically find in the back of the book? The *answers*—usually to the even or odd numbers. Let's say you work out a problem and your answer turns out different than what's in the back of the book: most likely, which answer is wrong—*yours* or that of the *textbook*? So after noticing that your answer is different than that in the back of the book, you then proceed to re-work the problem. The answers are a guide, a check, but notice: *you still work out the problem*; so likewise, dogmas are never an excuse for sloppy thinking. Rather, the answers in the back of the book guide us, correct us, and impel us to further and sometimes innovative ways of reaching and better understanding the truth.

THE VIEW OF ST. JOHN PAUL II

In *Fides et Ratio*, John Paul II gives unflinching support for the legitimacy of Christian philosophy and actually takes it one step further than I laid out just now in the math book example. For him, there are two aspects to the notion of Christian philosophy, what he refers to as its *subjective* and *objective* aspects. The "subjective aspect" refers to what happens to the knowing subject whose reason is purified by the light of faith, much as in the "answers in the back of the book" analogy above;[6] knowing is not always (and perhaps seldom is) a purely dispassionate exercise where the person is not self-involved in the matter; rather—and especially with the preambles of faith—*these conclusions matter*; it matters a great deal who is right, and so there is always a complicated dynamic of intellect, will, and emotion—not to mention the effects of sin—upon our knowing endeavors (hence, the importance of "paradigms," as discussed in the introduction).

St. Paul made this point when discussing reason's ability to go from creation to the Creator, stating that from "the creation of the world [God's] invisible nature . . . has been clearly perceived" (Rom 1:20). But in the very same passage, St. Paul notes that men by their "wickedness" can "suppress the truth" (Rom 1:18). In other words, often the problem is not necessarily in the *intellect*, but in the *will*. So, faith here (in the *subjective* aspect of Christian philosophy) purifies the reason of the knowing subject, the person who seeks to know.

As for the "objective aspect," here is where St. John Paul II takes things a bit further; this aspect refers not first to the knower but to the *object* that is known: that is, the faith proposes objects of inquiry, certain ways to think about real problems, which are accessible to reason, in principle, but which were first proposed by faith.[7] Thus, the faith may open up new vistas for reason to consider, vistas which reason may never have come to on its own—had they not been first suggested by faith. So here, faith not only purifies the knower, but actually proposes further *objects* for reason to consider.[8]

---

6. Pope John Paul II, *Fides et Ratio*, 76.

7. Ibid.

8. As examples, the late pope writes, "Among these truths is the notion of a free and personal God who is the Creator of the world, a truth which has been so crucial for the development of philosophical thinking . . . . There is also the reality of sin, as it appears in the light of faith, which helps to shape an adequate philosophical formulation of the problem of evil. The notion of the person as a spiritual being is another of faith's specific contributions: the Christian proclamation of human dignity, equality, and freedom has undoubtedly influenced modern philosophical thought" (ibid.).

For my part, Wojtyła's 1960-work, *Love and Responsibility*, is a particularly good example of what he later described as Christian philosophy. For starters, in his introduction, he begins by noting that several biblical passages have played a critical role in informing his thought (Matt 5:27, 28; 19:1–13; Mark 10:1–12; Luke 20:27–35; John 8:1–11; 1 Cor 7; Eph 5:22–33).[9] He describes this "handful of most important statements" as a "frame of reference throughout."[10] Moreover, the importance of Christ as the supreme teacher of what it means to love—and indeed the supreme example of what it means to be human—is always in the background for John Paul II. So, clearly the faith informs his thought, but not at the expense of developing his own rational inquiry and analysis. His procedure in *Love and Responsibility* is still largely philosophical, developing a rational exposition and analysis of the human person and what this means for love and sexual love in particular; but this rational exposition has, no doubt, been nurtured and fostered from within the bosom of faith.

We see here the dynamic interplay of faith and reason in St. John Paul II; we will return to his teaching on love and sexuality in chapters 7 and 8. For now, let us move from John Paul II to Aristotle, as the title of this work has it. We will turn particularly to Aristotle's teaching on virtue, noting especially how it is rooted in the natural order, specifically human nature. My hope here is that the reader will see the importance of the framework of *natural* virtue and its connection to an analysis of human nature for providing a wider context for understanding the ethical life of the Christian; indeed, getting "nature" right and taking it as far as it can go does not take away from the sublimity of grace, but just the opposite. Further, this Aristotelian background often lies behind Wojtyła's analysis in *Love and Responsibility*, so the following is actually a necessary propaedeutic for understanding the later chapters on John Paul II.

9. E.g., "You have heard that it was said, 'You shall not commit adultery. But I say to you that everyone who looks at a woman lustfully has already committed adultery with her in his heart" (Matt 5:27).

10. Wojtyła, *Love and Responsibility*, trans. H.T. Willets, 16.

Now we move from Wojtyla, and this discussion of Christian philosophy, to Aristotle—of course, only to return again to Wojtyla by the book's end.

3

Moral Foundations in the Natural Order—Aristotle's Treatment in General

HUMAN NATURE, VIRTUE, AND HAPPINESS

WITH RESPECT TO ASSESSING what moral goodness entails, Aristotle turns first to the order of nature and to human nature in particular.[1] He asks, "What is man's proper *function*?" That is to say, what is man's purpose, *as* man? If we were to consider a watch, for example, we know what a *good* watch is in virtue of the watch's basic purpose or function, namely, to tell time; so a good watch is one that tells time *well*. For Aristotle, the same goes for man. He defines man as a "rational animal"—"animal" in this case being the larger category, and "rational" the specifying feature of man which sets him apart from other animals.[2] Now while animals do amazing things, and there are the amazing similarities in the genetic code between man and some of the higher animals, it is certainly the case that only *one* species is interested in studying the genetic

1. *Nicomachean Ethics*, Bk. I, ch. 7.
2. Ibid.

code of the other—we study the monkey's DNA, not the other way around! This should suffice for us to follow Aristotle's lead here.

As with the watch example above, Aristotle applies the analogy to man: a good man is simply one who lives according to reason *well*, since reason is what specifies our nature *as* man. What often impresses my students is how nimbly Aristotle moves from nature to ethics—from *what* man is, to what a *good* man looks like. In an era where moral discussion often seems like an arbitrary choosing of moral platforms (or paradigms) from which to scream at an opponent, this aspect of Aristotle strikes many as incredibly refreshing.

Because of the above link in Aristotle's thought between human nature and the human good, I often point out that Aristotle's teaching on "virtue" is very different from a typical discussion of "values." "Values" has an economic ring to it, since *demand* gives something value, not its intrinsic worth; and that means "values" ebb and flow with demand, making them as arbitrary and subjective as the fads of a given society. For Aristotle, on the other hand, virtue is *perfective of our nature*. In other words, acting in accordance with virtue and acting in accordance with right reason are two ways of saying the same thing. This is why the virtues for Aristotle are in a sense *one*, namely, living in accordance with right reason; the virtues are diversified only when we consider reason's application to different aspects of life.

Many have heard of the "cardinal virtues." This name comes from a Latin word *cardo* which means "hinge." These are the virtues upon which human life hinges: prudence, justice, courage, and temperance.[3] But for our part now, let's take notice of the fact

3. Aristotle's treatment is slightly different; he first treats virtue in general and then courage and temperance (second half of Bk III); then justice (Bk V); and then with the intellectual virtues, he treats prudence (Bk VI). The intellectual virtues are divided into two groups: those ordered toward *knowing* and those ordered toward *doing*; the former consists of understanding, science, and wisdom; the latter, of prudence and art. One can see how prudence straddles both the moral and intellectual virtues: it is intellectual because it rooted in the mind, but it also has a moral component because it is ordered toward moral action. As we will see throughout, these virtues are perfective of our nature because they perfect the specific powers of human nature: intellect,

that these virtues become virtues precisely because they exhibit the part of right reason: when we allow right reason to inform our moral decision-making, we call it "prudence"; when we allow right reason to inform our dealings with others, we call it "justice"; when we allow right reason to inform our internal states with regard to the emotion of fear, we call it "courage"; and when we allow right reason to inform our bodily desires for food, drink, and sex, we call it "temperance." Notice, then, that the virtues don't fall out of a hat; Aristotle is simply moving from *what* we are as human beings (rational animals), to an analysis of what it means to be a *good* human being: a good human being is one who lives according to his nature *as rational*; the virtues are simply those habits that enable us to live the fully *human* life, to live in accordance with right reason.

The virtues, then, enable us to get the most out of life. As an analogy, what's the first thing that happens at a Mexican restaurant (my favorite restaurant food, by the way!)? They bring you chips and salsa; and if you're like me, you find yourself quickly asking for another basket, and then maybe *another* one after that. In due course, what happens when the meal comes out? If you're like me, you're full! And consequently, you're not as free to enjoy the meal. This is much like the virtue of temperance: if you fill up on the "chips and salsa" of life, you're likely to miss out on the main course.[4] In this light, we can see here that the acquisition of virtue, for Aristotle, is about reaching the human end of happiness—about a human life well-lived. It's about becoming the kind of person who is good and is able to fulfill his relationships, as father, husband, mother, wife, friend, teacher, doctor, etc. Virtues are the skills needed to live a life of excellence—to get the most out of life; and happiness, for Aristotle, is the fruit of a character which possesses these skills—that is to say, *happiness follows on virtue*.

Therefore, for Aristotle, happiness is less about something that happens *to* me, and much more the fruit of my character. We all want to be happy, but too often we pursue this as a merely passive search: if only *this* would happen to me—"*this* relationship,"

---

will, appetitive passions/emotions.

4. I have taken this example from my former teacher, Dr. Edward Sri.

"*this* job," "*this* college," "*this* exam," and so forth. Aristotle knew that these types of things are much too precarious to carry the weight of the human heart. Happiness, rather, is something we are much more in control of precisely because it's the fruit of our character; and therefore, it's not something we're simply "waiting for," nor is it something that can be easily taken away; it is something internal—it is due to our character, and for this reason Aristotle can say, "No happy man can become miserable."[5]

VIRTUE AS A STABLE DISPOSITION

This may well sound nice, but perhaps much too lofty ever to be realized; for just how does one actually begin to acquire virtue, these human skills which bring about happiness? The key is his notion of "habit" or a stable disposition; for him, the moral life is about much more than simply external actions; it's about becoming a certain kind of person. Here is the basic principle for Aristotle: *like acts develop into like habits.* This means that the more I perform a certain kind of action, the more it becomes ingrained within me, a "second nature," as it were; this is very important—for if we follow him here, we will see that our actions are not disconnected from the kind of person we are becoming; indeed, in each and every act, we are modifying and forming our very selves.

This habit-forming nature of our actions over the long haul pertains to both virtue and vice; if virtue is a good habit, perfective of our nature as rational, then vice is a bad habit—one which ultimately de-humanizes and thwarts the human good; that is, vice leads to unhappiness. The point here is that the more you feed a habit, whether good or bad, the stronger it gets; and as the habit grows, the more one is inclined to act likewise the next time; and so the cycle continues—reinforcing the habit, and disposing one to like acts in the future.

In order to understand what Aristotle is getting at, let us turn to analogies closer to home, such as: getting in shape; learning a

---

5. Ibid., Bk. I, ch. 10.

musical instrument, or a foreign language; or mastering any kind of athletic skill where at first it feels awkward and clumsy, but eventually gets easier and easier (e.g., shooting form in basketball, mechanics of a pitcher, or perhaps a golf swing). With all of these, we can see that the more one practices the sought-after skill, the more one grows in one's ability to perform that skill consistently and with ease—and we even tend to enjoy such skills more, the better we get at them.

PLEASURE AND PAIN AS INDEX OF CHARACTER

In this light, let us consider the following strange but profound comment from Aristotle: "We must take as a sign of [our] state of character the pleasure or pain that ensues on acts."[6] He is basically saying that the pleasure or pain that accompanies an act is an *index of our character*. What does that mean? Well, consider a running analogy: if you were to run a six-minute mile (which for me is *really*, really fast!), and after completing it you threw up all over the place, what does this tell you about how good of shape you're in? You're probably not in as good of shape as you want to be; but if you were to train for a series of months and then run the same mile (same pace/same time), would the outcome be different? Well, surely, if you're in better shape, it won't be as painful to run the mile at the same pace as you did previously. And guess what? The better shape you're in, the longer and harder you can run, and the more you will enjoy doing so—much more so than you did before you got into shape.

This is exactly how Aristotle envisions the moral life; his comment above about pleasure and pain being an index of our character means this: if we're especially *pained* by the performance of some virtuous action, then we have not yet mastered that particular virtue; that's why he says that the pleasure or pain that accompanies or follows an action is a sign of our character—it's a sign of how far along we are in terms of attaining that particular virtue.

6. Ibid., Bk. II, ch. 2.

We can see here that Aristotle's whole ethical program is not simply about obeying rules; it's not simply about being compliant with respect to our duties; it's about becoming the kind of people who not only do the right thing, but actually *enjoy* doing it; morality is about our moral growth so that we can become truly *happy* people—something interior as the fruit of our character, and therefore, again, something which cannot easily be taken away.

A GREATER FREEDOM

The above discussion leads to a whole different conception of freedom than the one we're used to as good Americans; in order to kick this discussion off, I often ask my students if any of them speak French; and then I ask those who did *not* raise their hands whether or not they are *free* to speak French? They invariably say, "Yes," looking at me with mild amusement; then I respond, "Ok, go ahead—speak some French." And then they remind me that they have not had French and therefore they cannot speak it fluently at the moment—to which I reply, "But I thought you said you were *free* to do so."

You see there are two different kinds of freedom; there is the *freedom to do what I want, when I want*; this is basically the freedom to choose, freedom from constraint. This is an important part of freedom, no doubt; and it's at the heart of the American dream of individual liberty. But I always seek to impress upon my students the fact that there is something more, namely, *freedom for excellence* which means having the *ability* to do the good.[7] What's important about this freedom for excellence is that it's not an all-or-nothing prospect like the freedom simply to choose; that is, freedom for excellence can *grow* over time. The more I practice, the freer I become; the freer I become, the more I have the ability to be the person I truly long to be—the freer I am, therefore, to be truly happy.

7. See the chart found in Pinckaers, *The Sources of Christian Ethics*, trans. Sr. Mary Thomas Noble, 375.

A former teacher of mine, Fr. Robert Barron, captured this kind of freedom as follows: *freedom is the disciplining of desire so as to make the achievement of the good at first possible, and then effortless.* Notice that the goal of the virtuous life, then, isn't "always to do the hard thing"; rather, it's to become the kind of person who does right thing *effortlessly.*

I know this sounds like a hard climb—like it's really not possible—but consider the amount of time and energy we have put into subjecting our bodies to attain some kind of athletic excellence or prowess; or, consider the amount of time we have put into attaining certain academic accolades or honors. Can we really say that we have put this kind of effort into the training of our souls, the attaining of moral excellence? For most of us, the answer is likely no; and the reason is because, for most of us, morality is about following certain rules, or at least not breaking the ones that would make us "really bad." But imagine if I were a basketball player and I said, "Ok, I'm not going to foul; I'm not going to dribble the ball out of bounds; I'm not going to break any rules"—would I be any good? Probably not; this would be *playing not to lose*—the death knell of any tournament run come March, as any basketball fan will tell you. Rather, if you want to be a great basketball player, you've got to master the skills—ball handing drills, passing form, shooting technique, mastery of the off-hand, etc. Only the person who subjects himself or herself to this kind of discipline and over the long haul can hope to become a truly great player on the court. This is what it would mean *to play to win.* The same is true in the moral life: abiding by the rules of the lowest common denominator is simply playing not to lose, with a very dim and tenuous link between the moral life and happiness; whereas the ethic of virtue is playing to win—playing to be great, playing to be truly happy.

THE TRUE MORAL QUESTION

The moral question, then, for us to keep before ourselves should not just be: "*What do I do right here and now?*" This makes it sound as if our moral lives are simply made up of discrete, disconnected moral dilemmas that span the course of one's life. Rather, the real moral question that always should be before us is this: "*Who do I want to be?*" The reason is because our moral lives are a journey, and all our actions are connected in a continuous plot. Recall the teaching that actions eventually become habits, which then incline us to further like actions. There is no stagnation in the moral life; either we're progressing or we're regressing; each and every action reinforces a habit, for better or worse. Don't let the simplicity of this teaching fool you, for it has profound implications. For example, the notion that "I should just live it up while I'm in college and settle down later when I get married" would be preposterous to Aristotle. My actions today are forming who I am; I am *becoming* a certain kind of person—and this plays out especially in the little things. This is to say, then, that the person I am five years from now is *directly* related to what I am doing today.

Indeed, at a point *my actions dictate who I am*. I know this may sound harsh, since we're so used to disconnecting our actions from who we are deep inside (i.e., "deep down I'm a good guy, despite what I did last weekend"). But consider this statement: "*Deep down I'm a good pitcher; I just never throw strikes.*" That would be nonsense; and the reality is that each and every pitch I throw with poor mechanics makes it more likely that my mechanics will be off the next time. My prayer is that you see that this virtue-ethic invests the littlest moments of life with the utmost significance: do I make a habit of giving into my desires and letting them overcome me in the small things? How hard would it be for me to go through, say, one meal a day denying myself just one thing that I typically enjoy having (ketchup, salt, etc.)? Each and every moment is a training ground; if we want to be the hero when it counts, our best hope is to have fought the good fight in the little things along the way, getting us into "moral shape" and making us freer to be more reliable in the future. After all, isn't this why coaches constantly harp "*You play how you practice*"? This is true in athletics; it is true when trying to learn a foreign language (one must learn it the right way early and often); it is true with regard to a musical instrument; and it's all the *more* true—not less—in the moral life.

Here we have laid out the basic Aristotelian framework for ethics—an ethics of good habits (virtues) which are built up and acquired over time and which then lead us to our end of happiness. This notion of habit invests the "small" moments of life with great meaning over the long haul; and it introduces a more profound type of freedom—the freedom to grow in one's ability to do the good. This freedom for excellence, acquired through discipline, puts us on the path toward happiness, a happiness which is ultimately much more the fruit of our character, than simply the circumstances that happen to us, or a merely some state of contentment.

In the next chapter, we will take this analysis further, treating more specifically the virtues of courage, temperance, and prudence.

4

From Nature to Virtue—Specific Aristotelian Applications

IN THIS CHAPTER, WE hope to make this virtue teaching a bit more concrete; what follows below will tie back into the previous chapter, in terms of virtue being perfective of our human nature as rational, but here we will go a bit further into what a virtuous act looks like and how to grow in the virtues personally.

Aristotle defines virtue in general as a "rational mean" between two extremes.[1] This definition will apply most aptly to courage and temperance, and the reason is that these virtues are in some ways the most appropriate to our human nature. What I mean is this: there have been many treatises throughout the years on God's Justice, but not on God's Temperance; and the reason is because God doesn't have a body, or bodily desires the way we do; the same is true with regard to courage. But these two (courage and temperance) are especially appropriate to us, since we are rational *animals*—that is, we are *embodied* persons.

1. I am paraphrasing a bit here; this definition can be found in Bk. II, ch. 6.

COURAGE

Let's begin with courage; it's the "mean" (the middle) between two extremes—the extremes on either side being "cowardice," which is the vice most opposed to courage, and "rash boldness" on the other side. In this analysis, "courage" would be the virtue; "cowardice," the opposing vice; and "rash boldness" the counterfeit vice. A counterfeit vice is something that looks like the virtue but isn't when all is said and done. Now notice that there is a strange commonality in both cowardice and rash boldness, namely, that in both instances one is governed by emotion—by fear (with regard to cowardice), or by rage or anger (with regard to rash boldness). In both the vice and the counterfeit vice, one is acting in a less-than-human way—in a way that is not fully in accord with the good of human nature, not fully rational—and therefore, not virtuous.

The key to courage is that it's not *not* having fear; it's not letting fear control or paralyze you. Similarly, on the other side, passions of anger need not be bad in themselves, but the question is what plays the governing role in my action—reason or emotion? If emotions are subordinated to the direction of right reason, they are wonderful; when emotions lead, our moral lives enter into disarray and we begin to lose control.

For these reasons, Aristotle can call virtue both a "*mean*" (middle) and an "*extreme*."[2] Virtue is a mean between the two extremes of vice (e.g., cowardice) and the counterfeit vice (e.g., rash boldness); but virtue is an extreme with regard to "*what is best and right*."[3] Virtue is an extreme insofar as it is the most *human*, the most *rational*, course of action. Virtue, then, is like hitting the bulls-eye; and indeed, the word "sin" has an archery meaning to it: to be three rings out from the bulls-eye is to be three "sins" away. In fact, the Greek word translated as "sin" in the New Testament (*hamartia*) has the literal meaning of "to miss the mark."

---

2. Bk. II, ch. 6.

3. Ibid., emphasis added.

TEMPERANCE

The same analysis applies to temperance; the vice most opposed to this virtue would be "self-indulgence"; but Aristotle puts forth a counterfeit vice which he calls "insensibility." A life of self-indulgence is obviously not perfective of human nature, since it allows bodily passions and emotions to dominate, making moral choices more on the level of animals and not living up to the dignity of human nature as rational. But on the other hand, "insensibility" would be the attitude that sees the body and pleasure as intrinsically evil; this attitude subtly wishes one did not have a body to deal with—as if one secretly wished one were pure spirit with no body. This is absolutely *not* the Christian view, which—despite common opinion—actually relishes in the body; after all, the Son of God became man and took on flesh (cf. John 1:14); and the Apostles' Creed states, "I believe in the Resurrection of the body"; and historically, the sacraments have been understood by the church as the visible and bodily means by which the grace of the Risen Christ "touches" us in the ever-present in every generation.[4] Aristotle likewise insists on the importance and the goodness of the body; the goal for him is certainly not to see pleasure as an evil; rather, it is to place bodily pleasure and its pursuit within its proper context, its proper place, and its proper time—informed by right reason, not driven by blind passion.

My hope is that you see here how right reason informs all of the virtues; living virtuously and living in accordance with the fullness of our human nature (and living in accordance with right reason) are all ways of saying the same thing. And therefore, as we said earlier, *virtue perfects human nature*—it enables us to live human life to its fullest potential so that we get the most out of life; and in this framework, *morality is about happiness*—not a fleeting happiness, but one that is the fruit of a stable character which cannot easily be taken away.

---

4. See CCC 1015 where the Catechism cites Tertullian who states, "The flesh is the hinge of salvation."

PRUDENCE

Let us now turn to prudence because it has been called the "charioteer" of the virtues—and rightly so, since one has to have prudence in order to make good moral decisions; prudence, for example, guides one in discerning what the courageous action would be in this or that moment.

Prudence has two key aspects, a *cognitive* (knowing) aspect and a *deciding/action-oriented* aspect.[5] One has to allow reason to govern and inform the will as to which path one ought to follow; but then one has to follow through and execute the plan that reason has come to. Here we can see the inter-relation of all the virtues—for example, of prudence on the one hand, and courage and temperance on the other.[6]

While prudence has to lead the way, how likely is it that I will be able to execute sober and rational decisions if my passions and emotions are all over the place? In other words, if I do not have the virtues of courage and temperance, then my desires will not be subordinated to and aligned with right reason. In this sense, my lack of courage and temperance will inhibit my ability to be prudent because the dominance of my passions will often lead me to "rationalize" bad behavior. After all, when reason and emotions are at odds—which typically wins out? Do we usually realign our emotions in accordance with right reason, or do we typically cook up some good reasons to justify our emotions and desires? For most of us, it's usually the latter.

Further, suppose I lack severely in courage and confidence; but suppose I excel at the cognitive aspect of prudence; if I don't have the courage to carry out the dictates of prudence, then what good does it do? My lack of courage will inhibit my ability to

---

5. "Prudence is right reason applied to action . . . . Now there are three such acts [of prudence]. The first is to take *counsel* . . . . The second act is to *judge* what one has discovered . . . . But the practical reason, which is directed to action, goes further and its third act is to *command* which consists in applying to action the things counseled and judged." *ST* II–IIae q. 47, a. 8.

6. See McInerny, *Ethica Thomistica*, 107 where he discusses a "virtuous circle" between prudence and the moral virtues of courage and temperance.

exercise prudence, since prudence is not just about *knowing* (the cognitive aspect), but is ordered to *action*—that is, the following through and carrying out of the good action that my mind has come to.

And like the above-virtues, prudence can be understood in terms of the virtue/vice/counterfeit vice breakdown above. The vice to which prudence is most opposed is "impulsiveness." If we are impulsive in our decisions, we are led by our emotions; we are then not acting the part of a *rational* animal. But on the other side, there can be a "false prudence" which is overly cautious and afraid to commit to a decision. As we said, prudence is ordered to action; if one deliberates forever, but fails to act—then *one fails to act prudently*. Here is the counsel of St. Thomas Aquinas who read and studied Aristotle intensely: "One needs to *deliberate slowly* but *act quickly*."[7]

One needs to seek counsel and pursue discernment and reflection before acting; typically, a good test case is this: if you really don't want anybody to find out what you're doing—especially, if you don't want the people whom you respect the most to find out—then you're probably not acting in accordance with prudence. But once we've come to what prudence calls for, we must carry out the action promptly and decisively.

While our emotions and passions should never lead, once we've come to the good that we ought to do, we should actively harness all of our emotional energy in pursuit of that good. If one is angry at an injustice, for example, that anger may help propel one into action; this is good and even wonderful, provided that reason leads; reason must be in the driver's seat; but that said, something would be missing if the energy of emotion were left out.

GROWING IN VIRTUE

Sometimes I've been asked, "Which virtue should I work on first?" My answer is simply that to work on one is to work on them all;

---

7. *ST* II–IIae, q. 47, a. 9. Emphasis added to translation.

either grow in all of them or grow in none of them. Remember, the virtues are *one* in that they are simply allowing right reason to inform our lives; they are diversified when we apply right reason to different aspects of human life: to moral decision-making (prudence); relations with others (justice); to our emotional life of passions and desires (courage and temperance). Let us turn now to a few practical steps for growing in virtue.

The best way to overcome a particular vice is to practice the opposite virtue. It might seem like it would be possible to simply "stop doing" whatever vice one is struggling with, but it just doesn't work that way. You can't simply "stop" doing something; that vacuum has to be filled with a positive virtue. The best way to stop gossiping, for example, is *not* just to not do it, but to make a concerted effort to find something nice to stay about the very person about whom you're most prone to gossip.

This is where self-knowledge can go an awfully long way; different people are differently disposed to different vices and virtues; your struggles may well not be the same as someone else's. Part of Aristotle's general definition of virtue that I haven't mentioned yet is that virtue is the "rational mean *relative to us*." He certainly doesn't mean that it's all relative in the way people speak of moral relativism; what he means is that, for example, the temperate amount of food for a 13-year old girl is probably not the same quantity needed for a 25-year old man training to compete in the Olympics as a power lifter. The goal is still objectively the same always and everywhere: namely, the mean of right reason; but the exact quantity of food will obviously vary.

What this means in terms of self-knowledge is as follows: if one is personally more drawn toward cowardice by default, then that person needs to err a little on the side of being a bit more daring (toward the rash boldness side). If one were to imagine a stick that is bent in one direction, and one wanted to get that stick back to the middle, then one would need to bend the stick *past* the middle in order to get it *to* the middle. So, too, with the attainment of virtue: if one is naturally drawn toward one vice or another, one needs to err past the middle on the other side, so as to bring one back to the rational mean (i.e., the virtue). So, if one tends to err on the side of being overly rash, then one needs to aim more toward the side of caution.

SUMMARY AND CONCLUSION

By now we have a basic working framework of the relationship between man as a rational animal and the virtues which directly flow from human nature and perfect human nature—that is, in other words, the virtues which enable us to live the fully human and rational life. Since virtue is a habit, there is a significant distinction between *performing a (single) virtuous act* and *having a virtue*; the latter refers to a habit, a stable disposition inclining one to respond to any given situation in one way rather than another. For this reason, as we have seen, acquiring a certain virtue is the fruit of many like acts over the long haul; in this chapter, we have also seen that the best way to overcome a bad habit is to practice the opposing virtue.

Now that we have this basic framework in place, with a more specific working knowledge of the role of prudence, courage, and temperance and their inter-relationship, let us turn to some aspects of the Christian moral tradition, specifically, the seven deadly sins; here we will see the Christian tradition going beyond—but not against—this basic Aristotelian foundation, complementing and supplementing the teaching of the great Greek philosopher.

5

Christian Appropriation of the Virtue Tradition and the Seven Deadly Sins

IN WHAT FOLLOWS, WE will take up some of the ways in which the Christian tradition has subsumed and enhanced this virtue teaching of Aristotle, this "gift of Athens," as it were. The Christian tradition had no problem absorbing this virtue tradition and placing it in the context of the drama of sin and salvation in Christ.[1] For example, consider the theological virtues of faith, hope, and charity: if prudence is seeing the world as it really is, faith enables the believer to see the world the way God sees it; if faith heals, perfects, and elevates the intellect, consider how much hope heals and elevates the natural virtue of courage; consider, too, how charity goes beyond justice and how it purifies temperance, placing all things in the context of love of God and neighbor.[2]

---

1. See MacIntyre, *After Virtue*, 165–80. See also Kreeft, *Back to Virtue*.

2. We should also note here the importance of the infused moral virtues in the Thomistic tradition. Here we see grace healing and perfecting the *natural* order, an important prerequisite to grace's elevation and transformation of human nature. See Cessario, *Introduction to Moral Theology*, 93, 197.

In what follows, we will treat the seven deadly sins, with the aim of showing how this wrinkle from the Christian tradition easily complements Aristotle's basic teaching. These sins destroy the life of grace in our souls and they snuff out the joy in our heart; they are: pride, avarice (greed), envy, wrath, gluttony, sloth, and lust. Not only are these habits sinful, they set up considerable roadblocks in our search for happiness. And so to a consideration of each of these we now turn.

PRIDE

Pride is said to be at the root of every sin because it's fundamentally selfishness, the radical assertion of our self-will. In other words, "pride" here is not how you feel after a job well done; pride here is making oneself the center of the universe, as if the world revolved around me; it is *me-centered* and decidedly not *other-centered*.[3]

We see something of this going on in the Bible's account of the fall in Genesis 3. Given that the Hebrew word "to know" (*yada*) connotes a sense of intimacy—not just intellectual knowledge,[4] the temptation of the "tree of the knowledge of good and evil" where man could come to "*know* good and evil" and become "like God" may well refer—not to knowing (or recognizing) good and evil, but to making oneself the *arbiter* and *determiner* of good and evil. At issue, then, is the basic question of whether or not man will accept his place as *creature*—or, if he will resent his creaturely status and attempt to usurp for himself the role of God.

To *recognize* good and evil is to come face-to-face with a pre-existent order—a moral order, akin to the order embedded in the universe which is studied by the scientist, as mentioned in chapter 1. This is the temptation then: will man conform his life to

3. Cf. "Freedom . . . uprooted from any objectivity is left to decide by itself what is good and what is evil. This relativism becomes, in the field of theology, a lack of trust in the wisdom of God, who guides man with the moral law." Pope John Paul II, *Veritatis Splendor*, 84.

4. In Genesis 4, on three occasions, "to know" is used euphemistically to refer to the marital act (4:1, 17, 25).

an order already present, given by God; or, will he reject his status as a creature and attempt to make himself the arbiter and creator of good and evil? In this respect, the philosophy of Friedrich Nietzsche—whereby our wills *create* good and evil as mere social constructs—is diabolical indeed.[5]

To reject the truth of the natural order—moral, scientific, etc.—is to reject the embodiment of divine wisdom; this thirst for absolute autonomy seeks to displace the Creator. And when this selfishness removes God from one's moral universe—making oneself the center—the trampling of fellow human beings is usually not far behind. After all, there can only be one "center" of the universe.[6]

WRATH

While we spoke of anger above, "wrath" here is different than simply the basic emotion of anger. The key ways in which the Christian tradition sees anger turning into "wrath" is when anger is (a) inordinate, an overreaction; or (b) harbored as a grudge over an exaggerated length of time. Thus, anger becomes the deadly sin of wrath when it is *disproportionate*, either in intensity or duration. This obviously varies with circumstances in terms of how much is too much, but it is something to take to prayer; unfortunately, anger, all too often, erodes the peace within our own heart far more than it disturbs the one with whom we are angry.

Anger can be compatible with love when it moves us to redress a wrong, to correct an injustice. But when anger moves away from redressing a wrong to simply hatred for the person, we've entered the realm of wrath as the deadly sin. For those who've suffered something truly heinous at the hands of another, the only

5. See Nietzsche, *Beyond Good and Evil*, trans. Helen Zimmern, 152: "*The real philosophers . . . are commanders and law-givers . . . .* Their 'knowing' is *creating*, their creating is a law-giving, their will to truth is—*Will to Power.*" Emphasis original in translation.

6. See de Lubac, *The Drama of Atheist Humanism*, trans. Edith M. Riley, Anne Englund Nash, and Mark Sebanc.

answer can be prayer—to surrender all of ourselves to the Lord; for combatting these "deadly sins" is not the same as acquiring natural virtue and overcoming vice. The deadly sins require surgery from the divine physician; only he can fill our wounds and transform us from the inside out.

ENVY

Envy is a particularly poisonous vice; it is often equated with jealously but classically there is a distinction. It basically goes like this: jealously is *desiring the good* of another, while envy is *sorrow at the good* of another (or rejoicing at the misfortune of another).[7] Theoretically, jealously can be neutral; envy is always bad. To give an example, imagine I am a student and I am jealous of my friend's grades; I want to perform as he does. This "jealousy" may cause me to reflect on my less-than-stellar work ethic of late and could perhaps motivate me to imitate the good habits of my friend. In this case, my jealousy may lead me to strive after the same good another possesses in order to achieve the same level of success. But to take the same example, envy simply means that I can't stand the fact that he is succeeding. It's the attitude that says, "If I can't have it, I don't want anyone to have it." So, envy might lead me to stick a nail in his tire before school on the day of our final exam, so that his flat tire keeps him from being able to attend and theoretically leads to a lower score for him in the class.[8] Whereas, jealousy might try to imitate the good of another, envy plays a zero-sum game: if you're up, I'm down; and the only way for me to be up is for you to be down.

Envy leads to intense competition among friends and members of a community; no one is happy for one another *because envy is just the opposite—sorrow at the good of another*. It leads to insecurity and gossip. For obvious reasons, it is toxic to friendships and destructive of community.

7. See *ST* II–IIae, q. 36, a. 1.

8. Of course, this presumes that such a teacher will be so unreasonable as not to allow the poor student to make up the work!

We can see here in envy a principle true of all of the deadly sins: they corrode the joy in our hearts; they lead to misery, not happiness. Virtue, on the other hand, leads to happiness; it makes us other-centered—whereas, vice turns us inward, making life boring *and* sad.

SLOTH

I have always found sloth to be one of the most interesting of vices; as I tell my students, "it's my favorite deadly sin," tongue in cheek, of course. Sloth is basically *spiritual boredom*; it's been defined as "sorrow at the difficulty of a spiritual good."[9] Many people think of sloth as laziness, but that's not quite right; it's laziness about the highest things, the most important things.

Consider New Year's Resolutions: how long do they last? That's sort of how sloth works; we have grandiose ambitions, but then we realize that it's just too hard, so we roll over and die; and then we're *sad*. What then do we turn to? Often, we distract ourselves, and this is how sloth can be present alongside a life of hyper-business and activity. But deep down, there's boredom latent there. *Only people can be bored*—ever notice that? The cow isn't bored—it just looks that way. But people are *made for more*—made for greatness, to know the truth and to love the good; and especially to know the most important truths and to love the highest goods.[10] Anything less can't satisfy the human heart.

LUST

Notice that sloth and envy are intrinsically tied to *sadness*. They turn us inward and make us sad. So what do we do then? If not distractions, we turn to *comfort food*. Here's where gluttony and lust fit in. Man cannot live without joy; and if he cannot find it in

9. *ST* II–IIae, q. 35.

10. This comparison with the cow comes from Dubay, *Faith and Certitude*, 204.

virtue, in love of God and neighbor, he will look for it somewhere else; if one's heart is really famished, he or she will settle for anything—even if knowing full well that such a course of action will leave the heart yearning for more. I bring this up especially to offer some advice: if one is struggling with, for example, a pornography addiction, the answer can't be simply just not to do it; that might work for a day or two, but probably not for the long haul. One must reorient one's life and consider how perhaps spiritual sadness and emptiness may be leading to the outlet of pornography and lust. Attack the disease, not just the symptom.

And I'd also offer one more thing: consider any AA program; the first thing one must do is recognize one's brokenness. Sin, too, is like an addiction. The best way to overcome an addiction is to begin by recognizing one's brokenness and place yourself in the infinite mercy of God. The lie of the Devil is that you need to heal yourself *first*, and then approach God's throne of mercy; this is backwards: it's the sick that need the doctor and they need to go to him *precisely when they're sick.*

Interestingly, the word "*Satan*" in Hebrew means "to accuse." Satan is the accuser, always pointing out to us and to God that we are not "good enough."[11] His lie is to say that "we are too far gone—that we are beyond the reach of God's mercy." We must remember that "God is love" (1 John 4:16) and that we love God "because he first loved us" (1 John 4:19). In the midst of temptation, the Devil acts as our friend—he's our buddy coaxing us to play along; but after we acquiesce, he becomes our *accuser*, seeking to douse us in shame and keep us from approaching the infinite mercy of God. As the accuser, Satan declares to us: "You are too far gone; your sins can't be forgiven, *after all you've done*—and if even when you pretend to repent, you always fall back into the same patterns; *God knows you're not really sorry*, or else you would have stopped sinning by now." This is part of the multifaceted lie of the Devil, as tempter and enticer—and then following our sin, as accuser.

11. Cf. Zech 3:1–5.

AVARICE

Needless to say, the spiritual sadness and emptiness we are discussing easily leads to another outlet, namely, greed. St. Paul makes an outstanding observation when he notes that "covetousness . . . is idolatry" (Col 3:5). When we want something so badly that it consumes our thoughts, we have made that thing into a "god." When this happens, we are less and less free to love because we are more and more consumed by some distant fantasy. Once, again, this destroys the joy in our heart. Life becomes navel-gazing, only about me; and that's precisely when life becomes boring and empty.

Our desires have to be ordered, if we are to be free to love; if our minds are preoccupied with what we don't have, then we're frankly not "available" (mentally, or perhaps physically) to those around us. Perhaps the best way to overcome avarice (greed) is to foster an *attitude of gratitude*; a greedy person is decidedly not thankful for the blessings he or she currently enjoys. If we are genuinely grateful, we will at least mitigate our constant yearning for "more." And deep down, we know that "more" is never-ending. Let us also note that this need for "more" is not restricted simply to material goods: sometimes "more" is prestige, power, honor—a promotion, or anything of the like.

Contentment and gratitude are not at home in our culture of intense competition and ambition. While being the best we can be is prized in our culture (and rightly so), this drive toward greatness can erode the joy in our hearts, if left unchecked. A wise friend once counseled, "Mediocrity in all things, except Christ."[12] While this statement may seem jarring at first, it does offer some perspective—a perspective which takes into account not just the "here and now," but eternity as well. And "perspective"—God's perspective—is actually what we need if we are to curb our passion for consumption, and surrender to the Lord our own plans for self-aggrandizement.

12. This statement comes from St. Paul's Outreach missionary and director, Sam Schoenfelder.

GLUTTONY

The same that was said of lust above could be said of gluttony; after all, the analogy we pointed to was "comfort food." Here, let's just note that gluttony is more important than we often realize. If our character is predominantly shaped in the little things in life—those things we do on a regular and habitual basis—it's certainly the case that "eating" is perhaps the thing we do *most regularly*. In the act of eating, we have a chance to exercise rational control over our habits—or, we can let our appetites take control of us.

Practically, we might ask ourselves: when we eat, what receives the lion's share of our attention—the *food* or the *people* with whom we are eating? Dining—in a dynamic interpersonal way—is something unique to human beings;[13] it's an expression of our rational nature; and, therefore, we ought to think of the table as daily practice for the habituation of ourselves toward becoming the kind of people who learn self-mastery. After all, self-mastery is the prerequisite to heroic virtue and heroic love—one has to be able to put aside one's own wants and desires for the sake of the good and the other. Just like any athlete, this comes only as the fruit of discipline over the long haul.

Since pleasure—particularly, food and touch—has been with us since birth, our default mode leans strongly in its favor. For this reason, occasional fasting makes perfect sense: since our barometer is tilted toward pleasure, if we are going to recover the "rational mean," then, occasionally, we need to forego what would otherwise be legitimate, for the sake of re-training our appetites and re-aligning our otherwise default mode which so fervently embraces that which is most pleasurable.[14] Fasting need not be elaborate, but could be as simple as drinking water, avoiding salt for a particular dish, eating a smaller portion, or refraining from dessert. Small amounts of fasting on a quasi-regular basis will generally be more fruitful than going a whole day without eating, only to gorge oneself later on.

13. See Kass, *The Hungry Soul*, 161–92.
14. See Pieper, *The Four Cardinal Virtues*, 181–82.

SUMMARY AND CONCLUSION

There are many more avenues we could have taken, but I pray you have come away with a sense that the moral life is the great drama of human existence—that it is truly a journey toward happiness; and that we are *becoming* something along the way. Morality is not simply about external actions and rules; it's not simply about "doing the right thing." Rather, it's transforming ourselves into the kind of people who do the right thing consistently, effortlessly, and with joy.[15] This frees us to become the kind of people we long to be; it frees us to engage in the authentic friendship for which our heart longs. Think about it: a great virtuous friend is like a "workout partner," but in the game of life; one who is running the race with you and alongside you; and who loves you so much that he or she wants nothing more than for you to grow in excellence and virtue—for in this lies your happiness.[16]

As with anything, training is difficult, especially in the early-going; the beginnings of any discipline are awkward, clumsy, and something of a grind. But nothing worth having in life comes without a fight. And like anybody who has experienced the joy of mastering a skill, of working through the early goings of something hard—so, too, there is no crown more prized than that of virtue. Nobody who takes up this battle ever regrets it; and nor do their friends and family—for they are the immediate beneficiaries of a virtuous man or woman. Virtue frees man to love; and isn't that what life's about? We've shed blood, sweat, and tears on the field with our teammates—what's that effort look like in the game of life? We feel good after going hard at practice—why should we be surprised when we're depressed and sad, if we put forth less than a full effort toward achieving excellence in the things that matter most? For Aristotle, our happiness is much more in our own hands

---

15. See CCC 1803: "A virtue is an habitual and firm disposition to the do the good. It allows the person not only to perform good acts, but to give the best of himself."

16. Indeed, Aristotle spends two whole "books" (out of ten) in his *Nicomachean Ethics* on friendship (see Bks. 8–9).

than we might imagine. Happiness is not something that simply happens to me; it's the fruit of our character, of a life well-lived.

Shortly, we will turn back to John Paul II, looking more closely at *Love and Responsibility* in order to observe how Wojtyla absorbs and goes beyond this Aristotelian foundation. After all, man is not just a rational animal; man is a *person—made in the image and likeness of God*. And further, for John Paul II and for Vatican II: "*It is only in the mystery of the Word made flesh that the mystery of humanity truly becomes clear*."[17] In other words, Jesus Christ teaches us from beginning to end what it means to be human; this passage from Vatican II became a leitmotif throughout John Paul II's pontificate, the sentiments of which can be found in the opening of his first encyclical, *Redemptor Hominis*: "Jesus Christ is the center of the universe and of history."[18] These statements are all clues that while John Paul II certainly absorbed the moral foundation discussed above, the late pontiff's Christian faith took him well beyond it.

But before we do that, I'd like to share my story of faith; for the ideas written herein are more than an intellectual exercise for me. I believe they are truly life-transforming, and I know this personally, as my encounter with them dramatically altered the course of my life—and I am forever grateful. So, to my story—from football to faith—I will now turn.

17. *Gaudium et Spes*, 22. Cited in *Vatican Council II*, gen. ed. Austin Flannery, 185.

18. *Redemptor Hominis*, 1. Cited in Pope John Paul II, *The Redeemer of Man*.

6

My Story From Football to Faith

As I write here, I am struck by how a number of the ideas we have discussed actually formed me into who I am today;[1] suffice to say, when I set out for college I never dreamed I would soon be laying the foundations for becoming a professor of theology, and even writing on the surpassing attraction of human life lived to its fullest in terms of virtue, so different from our culture's typical conception of "having it all."

My college choice came down to one thing: I wanted to play football. I had a pretty solid high school career, earning MVP honors my senior year as a team captain, and taking runner-up in our league's player of the year. I accepted a scholarship to play at a small Catholic liberal arts college (Benedictine College in Atchison, Kansas) and I did fairly well my freshmen year, making the travel roster, as well as the even more limited playoff roster.

It seemed, at least on the outside, that everything was going as planned my first year of college. Still, even though I seemed happy, inside I knew something was missing. I was empty; my entire

1. A version of this story has been published in *I Choose God: Stories from Young Catholics*, ed. Chris Cuddy and Peter Ericksen, 113–18 and in "Finding the Way: My Journey from Football to Faith" *Kansas Monks* Spring 2014, vol. 9, no. 1.

demeanor revolved around how things on the outside were going—football, image, etc. I suppose looking back on it, I could say I was made for something more—but at the time, I didn't know it.

A FRACTURED IMAGE

This all came to a head just after my freshmen year came to an end; our football team played in an exhibition game in Paris, France shortly after my first academic year. At the time, I didn't really want to go—all I could think about was getting home in order to train for the upcoming season. But alas, God had other plans: in the second quarter of the game in France, I broke my fibula. More than the pain of the break was the fact that all that I was—and all that I had built up and relied upon—came crashing to the ground. I went into something of a depression, deciding that I would "redshirt" the upcoming season—since I didn't want to "waste" a year of eligibility without having had the summer to train.

When I arrived back to college in August for my sophomore year, I caught up with a professor whom I had gotten to know fairly well toward the end of my freshman year; in fact, he was a theology professor—I had taken him for a few courses required by all students (Intro to Theology and a Synoptic Gospels) the semester before I got hurt.[2] At the time, I was intrigued by the things he taught—I was intrigued by his conviction; I knew he had something I didn't. After my injury, over the course of the summer, something started to happen: what began as an intellectual intrigue in my head slowly began to seep into my heart. And so when we caught up at the beginning of my sophomore semester, I had *lots* of questions.

The next day I received a phone call from him; he mentioned that he was teaching a course entitled "Christian Moral Life"; he noted that it was "full"—but that if I were interested, he would let

---

2. The professor's name was Dr. Edward Sri who soon became a mentor and eventually the godfather of my eldest son, and to whom I dedicate this work.

me into the class; based on the questions I had brought to him, he thought it would be "right up my alley."

A WHOLE NEW VISION

On my end, I was already enrolled in 17 credit hours, all of which were classes I needed for graduation requirements. But I happened to be redshirting that football season (due to my broken leg—as I said, I didn't want to "waste" a year of eligibility without having had the summer to train); and because of that, I decided to take the class, bumping my load up to 20 hours. It's hard to explain, but that class changed my life; I walked into it thinking that the class would be about a bunch of "rules," "dos and don'ts" from the church, etc. But I couldn't have been more wrong. The class was about virtue, happiness, true freedom—many of the themes we've discussed thus far. I finally saw the link between my head and my heart: I was "empty" because I was made for so much more.

LETTING GO

At this point, it was clear to me, and I began to find myself gathered around a different group of like-minded friends, pursing life as Christian disciples. But there was still one thing I had not given over to Jesus Christ—and that was a relationship with a girlfriend back home in Ohio; nice girl though she was, it was clear that this relationship wasn't bringing either of us closer to the Lord.

I remember fumbling through some prayers around October of my sophomore year; I remember almost audibly saying, "God, no matter what you say, I'm not going to end this relationship." Once again, it's hard to explain, but by the end of that semester, I had the most unshakeable conviction and confidence in what I had to do: both for her sake and for mine, I ended the relationship that December.

Most of my high school friends couldn't even begin to understand what was going on inside of me; but I knew I had met

Jesus Christ—I had found something that I'd always been missing, but just never knew it until now. During that Christmas break of my sophomore year I had never felt more alone—*and yet more at peace*—in my entire life.

During the following spring it became more and more clear what direction my life would take; these new concepts and ideas—and a relationship with Jesus Christ—had changed my life. And it was a professor who was God's instrument in my transformation; had it not been for his faith, conviction, and willingness to share these amazing truths with me, I would not be where I am today. So, I set out to "pay it forward"—that's why I'm a college professor of theology today; and I pray that some of the ideas in this book may take root for others, as they did for me.

Later on I met the woman who became my wife. To this day, I believe that God was preparing me to meet her; she never had to wonder about the sincerity of my conversion because it happened entirely before I met her. In answering God's knock on my heart in the feeble way that I could, God outdid my "generosity" to him many times over. We are now happily married with three children (and our fourth son is on the way!).

I say all of this because in so many ways, my life would look very, very different had I not encountered the Person of Jesus Christ and had I not been exposed to the Aristotelian moral vision of virtue. My wife encountered these same ideas by the same professor, and there's not a day that goes by where our academic and spiritual formation doesn't come into play in terms of how we run our household and raise our children. I couldn't be more grateful. At least to me, these are more than ideas; they are revolutionary and have made my life so much the richer—many, many times over. I have found that Jesus Christ doesn't make you less than you are or would have been: he makes you the very best version of yourself—better than you could have ever imagined, and yet organically related to the person you always thought you knew.[3]

3. See Kelly, *Rhythm of Life.*

SOMETIMES CLOSED DOORS OPEN NEW ONES

For what it's worth, when I look back on my story, I'm in awe of God's providence; so many doors—both opening and closing—helped to make possible my encounter with Jesus Christ. Just to offer one more example that I haven't mentioned: I tore my ACL in my right knee in the last football game of my eighth grade season. This plays into my story significantly because before this injury basketball was by far and away my favorite and best sport. But when I hurt my knee and had to have knee surgery, I was forced to sit out my eighth grade basketball season. It was at this point that I directed my athletic focus almost exclusively to football; after all, for a while all I could do was weight train with my upper body while my knee was mending. Football at this point became number one for me, over basketball. I say all this because it was football that brought me to Benedictine College from Dayton, Ohio; and it was at this particular college that—through a certain professor, Dr. Sri—I met Jesus Christ. Had I never hurt my knee in the eighth grade, I likely would have attended a different college; and had I gone to a different college, I may well never have had my conversion to Jesus Christ. God is never outdone in generosity; when we give him our lives, we are often amazed at what happens next. And we never quite know what he has in store: in my life, key doors had to close (e.g., tearing my ACL, leaving a relationship) in order for news ones to open up.

In the next chapter, we'll turn more directly to John Paul II and his vision for the "personal" order, particularly as the human vocation to love comes into play in and through our sexuality. We will notice that Wojtyla builds upon and transcends the Aristotelian foundation discussed above. For my part, my conversion to Jesus Christ was a "yes" to a culture of life and a "no" to a culture of promiscuity. I realized that a "no" to immediate pleasure was in reality "yes" to so much more—and, for me, understanding what this "so much more" was all about had a lot to do with my encountering John Paul II's vision for love and the vocation of every human person, a vocation to make of one's life a gift to others. And so to this vision, we now turn.

7

The "Personal Order" in John Paul II

GIFT OF SELF

WHEN LIFE IS LIVED in an outward-focused way, it is more enriching; that is the vision of John Paul II—namely, that man's vocation is to make a gift of himself, just as Jesus has done for us. This focus on love as gift, making a gift of ourselves, brings us into what the late pontiff calls the "personal" order. The personal order entails a love that is other-centered—that seeks the good of the other, first and foremost. The antithesis of this love, for John Paul II, is not so much hate, as it is loving the other *for my sake*, not for theirs—that is, for what *I* get out of it, and not with the good of the other foremost in mind. Indeed, for John Paul II, the antithesis of love is not hate, but use.[1] On the other hand, being concerned with the good of the other, first and foremost, is the hallmark of love: "The greater the *feeling of responsibility* for the [other] person," Wojtyla writes, "the more true love there is."[2]

---

1. Wojtyla, *Love and Responsibility*, 28–31.
2. Ibid., 131. Emphasis added.

For John Paul II, the mystery of life and the mystery of love—the mystery of happiness—boils down to making our lives a gift to others—this is the "law of the gift," as he puts it.[3] In short, happiness comes through the gift of self; this is what Jesus Christ teaches us about the human vocation—a vocation to love: "Greater love has no man than this, that a man lay down his life for his friends" (John 15:13). The Holy Father's vision here certainly goes beyond Aristotle, but not against it—for training in the school of virtue is the prerequisite to being able to make a gift of one's life in love to another.

In the context of *Love and Responsibility*, Wojtyla lays out what this means for human love and human relationships. He elucidates different dimensions of love as they relate to the constitutive aspects of the human person—here we will focus on *sensuality* and *sentimentality*. We are not just pure spirits with no bodies—we are human beings, with bodies and emotions; and so these "sexual values" (sensuality and sentimentality) inhere *in* the person. Yet the person—as an entity of inherent dignity and value—is always more than just his or her sexual values.[4] Contextualizing these sexual values in a personalistic way—in a manner that takes into account the whole of the person—is what the maturation of love is all about.

3. See John Paul II, *Man and Woman he Created Them*, 178–88. See ibid., 176. Also: Pope John Paul II, *Veritatis Splendor*, 17: "Perfection [e.g., happiness] demands . . . maturity in *self-giving* to which human freedom is called" (emphasis added). And: Wojtyla, *Love and Responsibility*, 97: "The fullest, the most uncompromising form of love consists precisely in *self-giving*, in making one's one's inalienable and non-transferrable 'I' someone else's property" (emphasis added). Also no doubt of relevance is *Gaudium et Spes*, 24: "*[Human beings] can fully discover their true selves only in sincere self-giving*."

4. Wojtyla, *Love and Responsibility*, 41.

SENSUALITY

"Sensuality" is simply our ability to attract and to be attracted by the physical qualities of another; this physical beauty—dare I say "sexiness"—is not, of itself, bad or problematic.[5] But it quickly turns that way when divorced from the reality of the person—that is, when taken in isolation apart from the full reality of the *person, in whom* these values exist, as Wojtyla states here:

> The body is an integral part of the person, and so must not be treated as though it were detached from the whole person: both the value of the body and the sexual value which finds expression in the body depend upon the value of the person . . . . A sensual reaction in which the body and sex are a possible object for use threatens to devalue the person.[6]

This is the source of the late Holy Father's well known comment about pornography—that the problem is "not that it shows *too much,* but that it shows *too little*"; that is, pornography focuses on *one* aspect of the person (sensuality) and misses out on the totality of the person. It's not that the body is bad; it's that the isolation of the body apart from the context of the person *devalues the person* and makes the person into an object to be used for someone else's gratification, thereby treating the person as less than he or she truly is.

---

5. "Sensuality expresses itself mainly in an appetitive form: a person of the other sex is seen as an 'object of desire' specifically because of the sexual value inherent in the body itself . . ." (ibid., 107). See also: "Pornography is a marked tendency to accentuate the sexual element when reproducing the human body or human love in a work of art, with the object of inducing the reader or *viewer to believe that sexual values are the only real values of the person,* and that love is nothing more than the experience, individual or shared, of those values alone" (ibid., 192, emphasis added).

6. Ibid., 107.

SENTIMENTALITY

"Sentimentality," goes a little bit deeper than sensuality with respect to the value of the person; but for that very reason, it can be all the more deceiving; after all, when one person is using another sexually—even if they are both using each other that way—it's pretty obvious that such a "love" is quite superficial. Sentimentality, on the other hand, goes beyond the mere physical and includes the *emotional attraction* to the other. Now as with sensuality, there is nothing inherently wrong with sentimentality; in fact, this is how a loving relationship usually starts—with attraction, flirtation, and romance which, in John Paul II's words, provide the "raw material" for love.[7]

But we've all heard the phrase "in love with love."[8] As love begins to mature, or when we think it has, we have to ask ourselves: am I seeking the other person's good above my own? Is my love *gift love*, or is it *needy love*? Earlier in *Love and Responsibility*, John Paul II distinguished between *love as desire* and *love as good will*: the former seeks the other as a *good for my sake*; the latter, "love as good will," loves the other in such a way that one wills, first and foremost, *the good of the other*.[9] Love as desire is still *needy* love, in that it seeks the other as a good which "fills me up," so to speak; love as good will is *gift love* which puts the other above oneself.

INTEGRATION AND VIRTUE

The key for love to move beyond sensuality and sentimentality is *integration*. Just as virtue entails—not the suppression of the body or of emotion, but their right ordering—so, too, the "integration" of love occurs when the will harnesses the powers of attraction (sensuality and sentimentality) and subordinates them to the inherent value of the person, in whom these values exist. This is

7. See ibid., 160.

8. See: "For that person . . . is less the object than the *occasion* for affection" (ibid., 113). Emphasis added.

9. See ibid., 80–3.

where love as a virtue, as an act of the will comes into play, where the good of the other is placed above what I might desire, physically or emotionally. John Paul II writes:

> Love as virtue is oriented by the will towards the value of the person. The will, then, is the source of that affirmation of the person which permeates all the reactions, all the feelings, the whole behavior of the subject . . . . *Our concern is simply to bind these values [sensuality and sentimentality] tightly to the value of the person, since love is directed not towards 'the body' alone, nor yet towards [the emotional attractiveness of someone's masculinity or femininity] . . . but towards a person.* What is more, it is only when it directs itself to the person that love is love.[10]

In other words, the inherent value of the person, as such, must be clearly distinguished from the experience of particular values present *in* the person, such as their sensual and emotional attractiveness.[11] And the integration mentioned above aims to subordinate our desire for a certain experience to a love for the person as such and a concern for his or her welfare: "Love as experience," John Paul II writes, must be "subordinated to love as virtue—so much so that without love as virtue there can be no fullness in the experience of love."[12]

What John Paul II is calling for is not settling for a less intense experience of love, but actually just the opposite. The problem with purely sensual or sentimental love is that it misses the full reality of the person; but when this comes full circle and the sensual and emotional attraction is placed in the context of a love for the person—for *who* they are, not simply how they make me feel—then even the *experience* of love grows all the richer.

---

10. Ibid., 123. In other words, a "love" that focuses solely on the sexual values of the person (either sensuality or sentimentality) is directed—not to the person *per se*—but to an aspect of the person, an aspect which has now become the object of isolated affection or infatuation. By "isolated," I mean here in abstraction from the context of the whole person.

11. Ibid., 122.

12. Ibid., 120.

IDEALIZATION AND THE EXPERIENCE OF LOVE

Wojtyla points out, as I think we're all aware, that emotional love can be given over to idealization—"love goggles," as it were, that see things that aren't entirely there.[13] And all too often, as is common in youth, this idealization ends in disappointment, as John Paul II explains here: "The discrepancy between the ideal and the real often results in sentimental love fading or indeed changing into a feeling of hatred."[14] Ever heard the phrase, *a cynic is just a disappointed romantic*?

But notice in the following citation how Wojtyla describes the emotional experience of a mature love, one rooted in objective reality—the full reality of the person, with his or her strengths *and* flaws in all. Here we see the richness of a mature love:

> The emotion becomes serene and confident, for it ceases to be absorbed entirely in itself and attaches instead to its object, to the beloved person . . . . As a result the emotion itself seems to acquire new properties. It becomes simpler and soberer. Whereas that idealization of which we spoke above . . . is characteristic of purely emotional love—the emotions themselves tend to endow their object with various values of their own creation. The love for a person [on the other hand] which results from a valid act of choice is concentrated on the value of the person as such *and makes us feel emotional love for the person as he or she really is, not for the person of our imagination, but for the real person.* We love the person complete *with all his or her virtues and faults, and up to a point independently of those virtues and in spite of those faults.* The strength of such a love emerges most clearly when the beloved person stumbles, when his or her weaknesses or even sins come into the open. One who truly loves does not then withdraw his love, but loves all the more, loves in full consciousness of the other's shortcomings and faults, and without in the least approving of them.[15]

13. Ibid., 112. He continues, "Sentimental love influences the imagination and memory and is influenced by them in turn" (ibid.).

14. Ibid., 113.

15. Ibid., 134–35, emphasis added.

CHASTITY AND THE DEVELOPMENT OF LOVE

So how does love mature to such a sublime height? As we said earlier, there is a need to *integrate* the sexual values of the person (sensuality and sentimentality) into the full context of the person. For John Paul II, here is where chastity comes into play, as the virtue requisite for the maturation of true love. Chastity is decidedly not a "no," in his mind—it is not simply abstinence or even primarily a negative virtue.[16] For without chastity, we get absorbed into the sensual and sentimental dimensions of love; while in the short term this may seem and feel wonderful, what actually happens is that it *arrests the full development of love*—it hinders the full maturation of love. In other words, without chastity, we get lost in the particular values present *in* a person (e.g., sensuality and sentimentality) and actually—whether we realize it or not—never come into contact with the full reality *of* the person; we never come to love them for *who* they are, but stop at what they can do for us, either physically or emotionally. And so John Paul II explains the essence of chastity this way: "The essence of chastity consists in quickness to affirm the value of the person in every situation and in raising to the *personal* level all reactions to the value of 'the body and sex.'"[17] This "raising to the *personal* level" refers to our ability to *appreciate* sexual values—not ignore them—but also to not get fixated on them in isolation. That is, chastity allows us to *integrate* these sexual values into a *personalistic* context—that is, in the context of the full reality of the person.

Thus, chastity is a *friend* of love; the only way chastity is not the friend of love is if we reduce love only to its sensual and emotional (sentimental) dimensions.[18] But if we desire true gift love,

16. "This (mistaken) view of chastity explains the common inference that it is a purely negative virtue. Chastity, in this view, is one long 'no' whereas it is above all the 'yes' of which certain 'no's' are the consequence. The virtue of chastity is underdeveloped in anyone who is slow to affirm the value of the person and allows the values of sex to reign supreme" (ibid., 170–71).

17. Ibid., 171.

18. Ibid., 146: "Sensual or emotional reactions to a person of the other sex which arise before and develop more quickly than virtue are something less

whereby the union of persons is the fruit of a total self-offering from one person to the other, and where the object of our love is the full reality of the person, then chastity plays a pivotal role in enabling us to contextualize the sexual values present *in* the person (emotional or physical), as aspects *of* the person—thereby preventing these aspects from becoming *isolated* objects of our infatuation and affection, which as we have said, inadvertently causes our love to freeze at that level without taking deeper root.

Chastity frees us to love because it makes possible the integration of the sexual aspects of the person (sensuality and sentimentality) into the context of a love for the person as such. In this sense, chastity frees love to deepen and becomes with time the union of two persons—not just the union of two bodies, or just a shared emotional experience. And when this union of persons takes place through total self-giving—gift love, not needy love—then paradoxically the emotional experience and even the physical experience of love deepens and grows all the richer.

This is the vision of John Paul II, a vision ordered toward man's authentic happiness, as the fruit of making one's life a gift in love. And the only way to make this gift a reality is preparation in the school of virtue. Here, we see John Paul II subsuming the Aristotelian framework and going beyond it. As we'll see in the next chapter, in the context of human love, this dynamic is brought about by joining and synthesizing what Wojtyla refers to as the "personal order" and the "natural order." This synthesis ties together some of the material from chapter 1 (e.g., the natural order as the embodiment of divine wisdom), in conjunction with the vision of love laid out here. And so we now turn to develop this synthesis further.

---

than love. They are however more often than not taken for love and given that name—and it is to love thus understood that chastity is hostile, and an obstacle. We see then that this main argument against chastity—that it is a hindrance to love—takes insufficient account both of the principle of integration of love and also of the possibility of 'non-integration.'" For more on many of the ideas present in this chapter, see Sri, *Men, Women, and the Mystery of Love.*

8

The Personal and Natural Orders in Synthesis in John Paul II

JOHN PAUL II AIMS to forge a union between: (1) living in accordance with the Creator's intentions rooted in the *order of nature*, an order which is taken to be the embodiment of divine wisdom; and (2) living in accordance with the reality and dignity of who we are as *persons* who have a vocation to love in a total self-giving way (i.e., the personal order).

As to the first, John Paul II clearly sees a moral meaning in the created natural order, one which he readily admits is easier to see for one who believes in a Creator, but which is nonetheless still accessible by reason.[1] With respect to the subject matter of *Love and Responsibility*, it's as simple as it is difficult to live up to: when we inquire into the purpose of our reproductive organs, the evolutionary and biological purpose is surely to preserve the species; and in this context, it is fitting that sex—at least according to most accounts—is a more intense pleasure than eating: for eating preserves the life of the *individual*, while sex preserves the

---

1. "It is much easier to understand the power of the natural order and its constitutive significance for morality . . . if we see behind it the personal authority of the Creator" (ibid., 230).

species—that is, sex serves the greater good because it goes beyond the good of just the individual.[2]

THE NATURAL ORDER AS THE EMBODIMENT OF DIVINE WISDOM

For Wojytla, the biological order isn't just about biology; that is, especially for one who believes in a Creator, as we have said, the natural order is itself an embodiment of divine wisdom, as he states here: "The Divine Order includes not only the supernatural order but the order of nature too, which also stands in a permanent relationship to God . . . the Creator."[3] As we have noted, this view entails a robust philosophical view of the natural order, seeing it as much more than just molecules in motion—that is, much more than what is unveiled through the scientific method alone. Accordingly, John Paul II is careful to distinguish the "order of nature" from the "biological order," the latter here referring only to what can be gleaned by the scientific method:

> The "order of nature" and the "biological order" must not be confused or regarded as identical; the "biological order" does indeed mean the same as the order of nature but only insofar as this is accessible to the methods of empirical and descriptive natural science, and not as a specific order of existence with an obvious relationship to . . . God the Creator. This habit of confusing the order of existence [i.e., the order of nature as understood to express the purposeful intentions of the Creator] with the biological order, or rather of allowing the second to obscure the first, is part of that generalized empiricism [i.e., scientism, as mentioned in chapter 2] which seems to weigh so heavily on the mind of modern man . . .[4]

This reminds me very much of what Cardinal Schönborn said in his catechesis on creation. He pointed to a certain shift at the

2. *ST* II–IIae q. 154, a. 2.
3. Wojtyla, *Love and Responsibility*, 56.
4. Ibid., 56–7.

origin of the early modern period in the philosophy of René Descartes, a shift toward what Schönborn calls "power knowledge."[5] This shift represents a move away from a conception of knowledge which aims to behold the natures of things and take into account their intrinsic order and purpose, toward a view which sees nature as simply raw material for man to exploit through technological prowess:

> At that time, a new kind of knowledge was being sought—not what things are, what constitutes their "nature," or, to put it another way, what their "logos" is, the divine idea that is being expressed in them—but rather what we can make out of them for ourselves. This approach to reality is called "power knowledge" . . .[6]

When this notion of "power knowledge" is translated into ethics, man can no longer look to the natural order as a meaningful guide, with which to begin his moral reflection; in this framework of "power knowledge," where the natural order has no intrinsic meaning or purpose, there can be no "language" of the body, as John Paul II proposes. For this reason Wojtyla readily connects this type of "power knowledge" to the claim of radical ethical autonomy: "Now if man is master of nature, should he not mold those functions—if necessary artificially, with the help of the appropriate techniques—in whatever way he considers expedient and agreeable? . . . . The claim to autonomy in one's ethical views is a short jump from this."[7]

---

5. Schönborn, *Chance or Purpose:*), 154–56.

6. Ibid., 155. Here Schönborn cites Descartes in his *Discourse on Method*, part six: "It is possible to arrive at knowledge that would be very useful in life and that, in place of that speculative philosophy taught in the schools, it is possible to find a practical philosophy, by means of which, knowing the force and the actions of fire, water, air, the stars, the heavens, and all the other bodies that surround us, just as distinctly as we know the various skills of our craftsmen, we might be able, in the same way, to use them for all the purposes for which they are appropriate, *and thus render ourselves, as it were, masters and possessors of nature.*" Cited in *René Descartes: Discourse on Method and Meditations on First Philosophy*, trans. Donald A. Cress, 35. Emphasis added.

7. Wojtyla, *Love and Responsibility*, 57. In light of the wider issues under

What happens in this move is a shift away from contemplation and a sacramental understanding of creation, as the embodiment of divine wisdom, to making sheer utility the supreme aim; knowledge is now ordered—not to the beholding of the divine idea embodied in creation—but to technology, to the mastery of nature.[8] With this move, the Creator is set aside—gone is the concern for the "message of creation," the purposes embedded in the natural order that provide the foundations for how we ought to live.[9] Indeed, "purpose" can now only be artificially constructed from without by man's imposition, as John Paul II explains here:

> A freedom which claims to be absolute ends up treating the human body as a raw datum, *devoid of any meaning and moral values* until freedom has shaped it in accordance with its design. Consequently, human nature and the body appear as presuppositions or preambles, materially necessary, for freedom to make its choice, yet extrinsic to the person, the subject and the human act.[10]

But for Wojtyla, nature is always more than particles in motion; thus, our freedom is not absolute, but must order itself in

---

discussion, I will provide the full citation here: "Now if man is the master of nature, should he not mold those functions—if necessary artificially, with the help of the appropriate techniques—in whatever way he considers expedient and agreeable? The 'bioloigical order', as a product of the human intellect which abstracts its element from a larger reality [i.e., the fuller order of nature, as we have discussed] has man for its immediate author. The claim to autonomy in one's ethical views is a short jump from this. It is otherwise with the 'order of nature', which means the totality of the cosmic relationships that arise among really existing entities. It is therefore the order of existence, and the laws which govern it [which] have their foundation in him, Who is the unfailing source of that existence, in God the Creator" (ibid.).

8. Schönborn rightly points out the implications for the environment here. In other words, belief in a Creator actually gives much *stronger* reasons to be concerned for the environment; the created order is a gift which embodies the wisdom of God—failing to show concern for it is nothing short of ingratitude on our part as creatures and stewards of what is not in fact ours to begin with.

9. Schönborn, *Chance or Purpose*, 155.

10. Pope John II, *Veritatis Splendor*, 48, emphasis added. He then refers explicitly to the "moral meaning of the body" (ibid., no. 49).

accordance with the truth.[11] Indeed, John Paul II's beloved phrase, the "language of the body," is nothing other than a reference to *the moral meaningfulness of the natural order*, particularly as it is expressed in and through the body and human sexuality.[12]

SELF-GIFT AS THE NUPTIAL MEANING OF THE BODY

For Wojtyla, the sexual act *says* something with our bodies; it connotes a total gift of self, from one to the other. Here, in terms of the meaning and significance of the sexual act, the natural and personal orders converge, as the late pope writes in the following: "In the sexual relationship between man and woman two orders meet: the *order of nature*, which has as its object reproduction, and the *personal order*, which finds its expression in the love of persons and aims at the fullest realization of that love."[13] He insists that we cannot separate these orders,[14] and that to thwart, for example, the natural order will simultaneously undermine the personal order. That is to say, in other words, that ordering our actions in accordance with the natural order is actually prerequisite to the full flowering of love in the personal order.[15] Indeed, for John Paul II, they stand or fall together.

11. Ibid., no. 4.

12. See John Paul II, *Man and Woman He Created Them: A Theology of the Body*, 531–47. The late pontiff notes, "Concupiscence [man's inclination to sin] does not destroy the capacity to reread the 'language of the body' in truth" (ibid., 546, given originally as General Audience, February 9, 1983).

13. Wojtyla, *Love and Responsibility*, 226, emphasis original in translation. See also ibid., 67, 227, 230.

14. Ibid., 226.

15. "Deliberate exclusion of this possibility [of procreation] conflicts not only with the order of nature but with love itself, the union of a man and a woman on a truly personal level, in that it reduces the whole marital act to sexual 'enjoyment'" (ibid., 236). Similarly: "Sexual morality and therefore conjugal morality consists of a stable and mature synthesis of nature's purpose with the personalistic norm" (ibid., 67). And: "Sexual relations between man and a woman in marriage have their full value as a union of persons only when they go with conscious acceptance of the possibility of parenthood. This is a direct

Certainly, this defies the modern conception of things, which readily dissociates the unitive end of sexual love from its procreative end. But to get a glimpse of what Wojtyla is getting at, let us consider the following statements—namely, the radical difference between: "*I want to have sex with you*" and "*I want to have a baby with you.*"[16] The latter bespeaks a radical permanence and commitment not necessarily implied by the former. "*I want to have a baby with you*" says I want another "*you*" in the world—I want to raise a family with you, and I want *you* to be one of the primary influences upon my children. Whereas, "I want to have sex with you" need not mean any of these things at all.

The phrase "I want to have a baby with you" is consonant with the natural meaning of the sexual act. On the other hand, "I want to have sex with you" is likely not consonant with either the *natural* or the *personal* meaning of the act: it is dissonant with the natural meaning because the statement suggests a dissociation of the sexual act from its natural connection to the possible conception of a child; and it is dissonant with the personal meaning of the act because it sounds as if one is only concerned with the "sexual values" of the person, not the person itself—which would convey a utilitarian love, not the personal love to which we are called. We will come back to this issue by the end.

CATHOLIC SEXUAL ETHICS

Catholic sexual ethics flows from this dynamic interplay and unity of the personal and the natural orders, wherein the two stand together. As to the natural ordering of the sexual act, we can say that it entails the following more specifically: a sexual act is in accordance with the Creator's intended purpose when the act is

---

result of the synthesis of the natural and the personal order. The relationship between husband and wife is not limited to themselves, but necessarily extends to the new person, which their union may (pro-) create" (ibid., 227).

16. In the following I am very much indebted to the work of Janet Smith; much of her popular work is readily available in audio and download format at www.janetsmith.org.

the kind of act which, of its nature, is open to the possibility of procreation. This is not to say that each and every act must result in procreation; but it is to say that a properly ordered act must be the kind of act that could, in principle, result in procreation. Now, the timing of the act (say, if it's engaged in during an infertile time of the month), or the particular individuals involved (say, if one or other is infertile) does not change the essential nature of the act; here the sexual act is still the same in kind, regardless of whether or not some circumstantial accidents render it infertile. As long as the act is the kind of act that could, in principle, result in procreation—even if such a result is unlikely (given the particular persons involved, or the particular temporal circumstances surrounding the act)—it still conforms to the natural ordering of the sexual act to the end of reproduction.[17]

This analysis, then, would exclude as contrary to the natural purpose of our sexuality—and therefore contrary to the Creator's intended purpose—sexual acts such as masturbation, oral sex (not merely as foreplay, but as the completion of the sexual act), and homosexual acts.[18] The Catholic Church sees artificial contraception likewise: as something that disrupts the Creator's intended purpose of the act by thwarting its natural end.

CONTRACEPTION AND NATURAL FAMILY PLANNING

The Catholic Church has approved Natural Family Planning (NFP)—where, based on a number very reliable empirical

17. See *The Meaning of Marriage*, ed. Robert P. George and Jean Bethke Elshtain, 160–64. Robert George uses the language of "reproductive-type acts" to delineate the nature of a sexual act which is, in principle, open and ordered to reproduction—even if there is a defect (in timing or, say, in the particular individuals involved) which renders the particular act infertile.

18. I place the accent mark here on "acts," since in the Catholic understanding, there is no sin whatsoever in having a same-sex attraction. Sin only enters in when one acts upon this attraction by performing sexual acts which are intrinsically not open to life and which are therefore considered disordered, thwarting the natural end of our sexuality. See CCC 2357–2359.

measures, couples can discern when exactly they are fertile during each month and then choose to abstain on fertile days (or *choose* to engage in the marital act *on* fertile days, for the purpose of conceiving a child). While many view NFP as simply a Catholic form of contraception, John Paul II marshalled a series of arguments noting that—while the end result may be similar, the moral means are different, which changes the moral assessment of each. Moreover, the personal order is likewise affected, in that—for John Paul II—the contraceptive sexual act communicates something deeper: it signals a less than total gift of self and thereby hinders the full union of persons, since something is being held back, namely, one's fertility. Again, "I want to have a baby with you" implies a total gift of self; "I want to have sex with you" implies only "I want to have a good time."

When faced with the objection that NFP and contraception amount to the same thing, I usually respond by asking: "Then, why not just use NFP?" The response I get is usually something like the following: "That would be *totally* different—it would change everything!" To which I respond: "But I thought you just said they were the *same* thing."

This typical exchange subtly reveals that John Paul II may be on to something—that perhaps there is a real difference between NFP and contraception, a difference that may actually affect the love between the couples involved.

For John Paul II, NFP is superior to artificial contraception, both in respect to the natural order and the personal order. For starters, NFP *works with the natural order*, not against it. The natural order is such that each and every sexual act does not result in procreation; accordingly, NFP simply works *with* the Creator's natural order.

Further, the late pontiff asks which—NFP or artificial contraception—calls forth greater virtue? That is to say, which is superior—not just in terms of its being consonant with the *natural* order, but also with respect to the *personal* order? For his part, NFP calls forth greater self-mastery (since the couple must abstain during certain periods of the month—generally, 7–12 days or so), and fosters greater respect between the persons involved by working against a utilitarian mentality which is always lurking to assert itself, most especially in the area of our sexuality. In other words, with artificial contraception, sexual gratification is theoretically always available; and fallen human nature being what it is, the possibility of using one another sexually is always there, even (or perhaps, *especially*) in marriage. Needless to say, the prospect of this utilitarian mentality runs directly contrary to the personal order, as understood by John Paul II. Utilitarian love is not gift love, but seeks the other as a means to some other end, here for the end of physical gratification.

CHASTITY IN MARRIAGE
AND THE BENEFITS OF NFP

It's in this light that we can begin to understand why John Paul II shocked the world when he proclaimed the need for chastity *in* marriage. The key, of course, is that chastity is not just abstinence. As we have seen, chastity is the contextualizing of the person's sexual values (sensuality and sentimentality) in the context of his or her inherent dignity as a person. That is to say, then, that even in and through the sexual act, it must remain a thoroughly *personal* act—in which case, the act can never be reduced merely to one of sexual pleasure.[19] Sexual pleasure is the wondrous gift of the Creator, but it can't be the primary end in itself; rather, sexual pleasure is something that accompanies and enhances the total self-gift made in love to the other. If sexual pleasure becomes the sole end of the act, the person often becomes merely the *occasion* for an experience, and not the object of true love.[20]

This is a tall order, but in this light, NFP—so contends John Paul II—is morally superior and more befitting to our nature as persons than is artificial contraception. Further, NFP helps to

19. Wojtyla, *Love and Responsibility*, 169: "Chastity can only be thought of in association with the virtue of love. Its function is to free love from the utilitarian attitude."

20. Ibid., 113.

promote two things that are very important to marriage in general and are certainly in keeping with the personalistic order: (1) non-sexual intimacy and affection and (2) communication. As for the former, since there are infertile periods each month, it forces the couple to show love in other ways besides the sexual act. It likewise precludes each and every intimate touch from being one that simply leads to a sexual encounter; that is, it fosters romantic intimacy, at times, *for its own sake*, not just as a means to sexual consummation.

As for the second point above, one may wonder what NFP or artificial contraception has to do with communication? But it's not hard to imagine a couple who has decided to use contraception—perhaps wishing to delay children for, say, some three to five years—simply going about their way for the next three to five years, and perhaps not having that discussion again until the allotted time has gone by. An NFP couple, on the other hand, may be having this conversation every couple of months: for example, say, they're on a romantic weekend get-a-way and they realize they're in a fertile period and therefore must forego sexual intimacy; each might ask the other: "Now, why are we so concerned about avoiding pregnancy right now?" One might respond: "Well, you've been really worried about finances." Or: "Because you never help me with the kids we already have!" Or, perhaps: "Well, you've described how tired you've been lately, taking care of the other little ones." However, the conversation might go—for good or for ill—the important thing is that the sacrifice involved in NFP is likely to elicit this very type of conversation. And these conversations are essential to a healthy marriage. Thus, for all of the above reasons, Wojtyla contends that NFP helps to foster "a profound culture of the person and of love,"[21] in a way that contraception does not.

---

21. Wojtyla, *Love and Responsibility*, 231.

SUMMARY AND CONCLUSION

In sum, while NFP and artificial contraception lead to the same end result of avoiding pregnancy, NFP is seen as morally superior because: (1) NFP is more in accordance with the natural order; and (2) it is more in accordance with the personal order, by encouraging a *personalistic* intimacy between spouses in the following ways: *sexually*, by calling forth greater self-mastery by abstaining periodically and thus working against a utilitarian mentality which so easily seeps into the area of sexuality; *emotionally*, by calling forth non-sexual affection; and *communicatively*, by providing a natural impetus to have the important conversations every married couple needs to have on a regular basis.

Again, we refer back to the opposing statements mentioned earlier—"I want to have sex with you" *versus* "I want to have a baby with you": the former always carries the possibility of thwarting the personal order and can incline toward a needy/utilitarian love which seeks—not the person as such and his or her good—but some erotic or emotional experience, whereby the experience is the primary object sought, not the person. In such instances, as we have seen: "The person . . . is less the object of than the occasion for affection."[22] On the other hand, "I want to have a baby with you" strongly connotes a love that is a total gift of self, holding nothing back—giving everything, including one's very life seeds. In other words, it expresses the meaning of the body's language when engaging in the sexual act, and it answers to the call of the personal order, namely, to make a gift of one's life in love.[23] Whereas, engaging in the nuptial act apart from this total and permanent

---

22. Ibid., 113.

23. I take the "symbolic meaning of the body's language" to be drawn first and foremost from the natural end of the act, namely, the conception of a child. In the grand scheme of things, this is what the sexual act is for; and so if there is a moral meaning to the natural order regarding the sexual act, it must entail that the sexual act should convey the union of two who have entered into a permanent and committed embrace, the natural result of which is the conception of a child. Thus, the total self-gift of the two to each other tends by its very nature to be fruitful.

gift of self strikes a chord of dissonance: something is said symbolically with the body (i.e., total gift of self) which the persons involved don't really intend to convey. We have here, in the view of John Paul II, a "lie" told with the body—purporting to express something physically that is more than the persons involved really mean to say.

While the goal of the sexual act is certainly not to have as many children as is humanly possible,[24] what is so revolutionary about Wojtyla's teaching is his claim that—not only does contraception disrupt the *natural* end of procreation, but that it also thwarts the *unitive* end of the sexual act. That is, for his part, contraception signals a less than total gift of self, thereby hindering the full flowering of personal love: "I want to have a baby with you" expresses an irrevocable unitive embrace, far exceeding that of "I want to have sex with you."

In the last and concluding chapter, we will look again at where we've been. And drawing on our title—"John Paul II to Aristotle and Back Again"—we will recapitulate our claim that St. John Paul II is a model intellectual for Catholics beginning the third millennium, especially for those engaged in the church's call for a New Evangelization. Needless to say, his missionary zeal as a disciple is perhaps just as significant as his teaching.

24. Ibid., 57–61.

Conclusion—Retracing Our Steps and Moving Forward

IT IS FRANKLY REMARKABLE what Aristotle came up with more than three hundred years before the coming of Christ, knowing nothing of supernatural revelation. A thorough study of him helps us to see the heights to which the "order of nature" and the "domain of natural reason" can climb. As I pointed out earlier, we really don't help our cause when we look down upon our natural faculties, supposedly in order to exalt the realm of faith. Rather, the higher nature climbs, the higher grace will soar; the further natural reason contemplates, the deeper the icons of faith will take us into the mystery of God. That's why the study of philosophy is important, not just theology.

But as we pointed out in the beginning, it's a mistake to act as if we live in two separate universes—one of faith and one of reason, one of grace and one of nature. While the distinction between the two orders is necessary, we distinguish not in order to divide, but to unite; for the marriage of divinity and humanity—the marriage, if you will of nature and grace—is found in the Incarnate Word, in Jesus Christ. And into this nuptial union, all people are called.

In fact, according to Vatican II, the "save the date" has already been sent out: "For, by his incarnation," the council writes, "he, the Son of God, has in a certain way united himself with each individual."[1] And this is why Jesus Christ teaches us from begin-

1. *Gaudium et Spes*, 22.

ning to end what it means to be human; as great as Aristotle is, the truth he teaches must be absorbed into the one Who is Truth (John 14:6). And that's why John Paul II's teaching on the human person's fundamental vocation to make a gift of himself is so important. Here the late pontiff builds upon the Greek thinker but certainly goes beyond him.

For Aristotle, virtue is perfective of our nature; we are beings with intellect, will, and passions; and from this follows the virtues which perfect our faculties and realize them in accordance with our nature as rational animals. Virtue is absolutely vital and necessary. But perhaps, for John Paul II, virtue is not quite the end, but the means which makes possible the authentic gift of self which holds nothing back. Indeed, virtue brings about *self-mastery*— whereby our desires and passions are aligned with right reason—a self-mastery which makes possible *self-donation*, that is, the total gift of self. In and through this gift of self, we begin to recapitulate the image of the crucified Christ. This is why martyrdom has been seen by the Christian tradition as the completion of discipleship— imitation of Christ has always been the first principle of Christian spirituality.[2] But for most of us, this "martyrdom" likely won't entail blood; however, it will entail the daily death to ourselves—to our desires/wants, to the "me-centered" part of us all—that part of us so often preoccupied by the seven deadly sins. And in the "death" of this part of us, we find Christian perfection: when the Holy Spirit reproduces the life, death, and resurrection of Jesus Christ in and through us, in each and every aspect of our lives.

John Paul II in this regard can be a great uniting force for us all; there's been a lot of talk about the "New Evangelization" and it's typically defined as the "new mission territory" in which the church finds herself, needing to re-evangelize continents that have long had the faith, but have lost it over the last two hundred years or so. Might I suggest it's even something more—something

2. See Ignatius of Antioch's letter to the Ephesians, ch. 3 where he states, "I am not yet complete in Jesus Christ. For now I am just at the *beginning* of being a disciple." He says this as he is under arrest and being taken to Rome to be killed for his faith. Cited in *Ignatius of Antioch & Polycarp of Smyrna*, trans. Kenneth J. Howell, 77, emphasis added.

embodied in John Paul II: it's this spirit of intellectual, moral, and spiritual rigor—an enthusiastic rigor that is inherently zealous and missionary.

I think that what John Paul II represents in terms of the New Evangelization is the total subordination of all of our energies and faculties to the service of the Gospel. It's not about thinking less; it's about training the mind *more* rigorously; it's not an excuse for intellectual laziness, it's a missionary charter. All truth is anchored in the real and all reality participates in God, because God is the One who gives it being; and God has revealed in the fullness of time that his Son is the *Logos*, the Word, and so all truth takes on a Christo-centric dimension, whether natural or revealed.

I close, then, by repeating once again the way in which St. John Paul the Great began his first encyclical: "Jesus Christ is the center of the universe and of history."[3] Fashionable as the chronological markers of "BCE" and "CE" are, BC and AD—"before Christ" and "*Anno Domini*"—are not just happenstance temporal indices; they point to the One Who *is* the anchor of all reality—for we don't say Jesus *was*, but that Jesus *is*, because the Risen Lord is *alive*. As disciples, intellectually, morally, and spiritually—we can't but live with this great truth ever at the forefront of our minds and hearts. That to me is the spirit of St. John Paul the Great; and that same spirit is shared by all those who have answered his call for the New Evangelization, which has been revitalizing the church—and especially the youth—for quite some time. My own story, no doubt, is one of many like stories of a younger generation who have been compelled by his call to make a gift of our lives. It's an exciting time to be a Christian and a Catholic, and I feel blessed to be a part of it.

For my part, the most depressing moments in life come when we feel we've lost sight of the meaning and purpose of our lives. But when we see our lives as part of the great story of salvation— begun in the Garden and continuing way beyond the death of the last Apostle—our lives are then seen in light of the great tapestry of divine providence; a story in which we all have our own part to play—young or old—and a part that perhaps won't be played

---

3. Pope John Paul II, *Redemptor Hominis*, 1.

unless *we* answer the call. This grand view of things doesn't take away from who we are as individuals, but enriches the meaning, purpose, and genuine reach of our lives all the more—well beyond anything we could have ever imagined on our own.

I pray you take this journey with me—not just for your sake and your own happiness, but for the world as well: may the Spirit of Christ continue the great drama of salvation, won for us on the Cross, and which continues to touch and transform us in the ever-present, as he has done throughout the course of history and will continue to do so in the future.

Works Cited

Adler, Mortimer J. *How to Think about God: A Guide for the 20th-Century Pagan.* New York: Collier, 1980.

Aristotle: Nicomachean Ethics. Second Edition. Translated by Terence Irwin. Indianapolis, IN: Hackett, 1999.

Barr, Stephen M. *Modern Physics and Ancient Faith.* Notre Dame, IN: University of Notre Dame Press, 2003.

Barron, Robert. *The Priority of Christ: Toward a Postliberal Catholicism.* Grand Rapids, MI: Brazos, 2007.

———. *Bridging the Great Divide: Musings of a Post-Liberal, Post-Conservative Evangelical –Catholic.* New York: Rowman & Littlefield, 2004.

Beckwith, Francis, J. *Defending Life: A Moral and Legal Case Against Abortion Choice.* Cambridge University Press, 2007.

Catechism of the Catholic Church. Second Edition: Libreria Editrice Vaticana.

Cessario, Romanus. *Introduction to Moral Theology.* Washington D.C.: Catholic University of America, 2001.

Chaput, Charles J. *Render unto Caesar: Serving the Nation by Living Our Catholic Beliefs in Political Life.* New York: Doubleday, 2008.

Cuddy, Chris, and Peter Erickson, eds. *I Choose God: Stories from Young Catholics.* Cincinnati, OH: Servant, 2007.

De Lubac, Henri. *The Drama of Atheist Humanism.* Translated by Edith M. Riley, Anne Englund Nash, and Mark Sebanc. San Francisco: Ignatius, 1995.

Dubay, Thomas. *Faith and Certitude: Can We Be Sure of the Things that Matter Most to Us?* San Francisco: Ignatius, 1985.

Flew, Anthony. *There is a God: How the World's Most Notorious Atheist Changed His Mind.* New York: HarperOne, 2007.

George, Robert P., and Jean Bethke Elshtain, eds. *The Meaning of Marriage: Family, State, Market & Morals.* Dallas, TX: Spence, 2006.

Gregory, Brad S. *The Unintended Reformation: How a Religious Revolution Secularized Society.* Cambridge, MA: Belknap, 2012.

Hannam, James. *God's Philosophers: How the Medieval World Laid the Foundations of Modern Science.* United Kingdom: Icon, 2009.

Ideas and Opinions by Albert Einstein. Translated by Sonja Bargmann. New York: Wings, 1954.

Ignatius of Antioch & Polycarp of Smyrna. Translated by Kenneth J. Howell. Zanesville, OH: CHResources, 2009.

Jaki, Stanley. *Savior of Science.* Grand Rapids, MI: Eerdmans, 1998.

Kass, Leon R. *The Hungry Soul: Eating and the Perfecting of Our Nature.* New York: Free, 1994.

Kelly, Matthew. *Rhythm of Life: Living Every Day with Passion and Purpose.* New York: Touchstone, 2005.

Kreeft, Peter. *Back to Virtue: Traditional Moral Virtue for Modern Moral Confusion.* San Francisco: Ignatius, 1992.

Kuhn, Thomas S. *The Structure of Scientific Revolutions.* Third Edition. University of Chicago Press, 1996.

———. *The Copernican Revolution: Planetary Astronomy in the Development of Western Thought.* Cambridge, MA: Harvard University Press, 1957.

Lewis, C.S. *Miracles.* San Francisco: HarperCollins, 2001.

Marino, Gordon, ed. *Ethics: The Essential Writings.* New York: Modern Library, 2010.

Maurice Nédoncelle, *Is There a Christian Philosophy?* Translated by. Illtyd Trethowan. New York: Hawthorn, 1960.

McInerny, Ralph. *Ethica Thomistica: The Moral Philosophy of Thomas Aquinas.* Rev. Ed. Washington, DC: Catholic University of America Press, 1997.

MacIntyre, Alasdair. *After Virtue.* Sec. Ed. Notre Dame, IN: University of Notre Dame Press, 1984.

Nietzsche, Nietzsche. *Beyond Good and Evil.* Translated by Helen Zimmern. Amherst, NY: Prometheus, 1989.

Pieper, Josef. *The Four Cardinal Virtues.* Notre Dame, IN: University of Notre Dame Press, 1966.

Pinckaers, Servais. *The Sources of Christian Ethics.* Translated by Sr. Mary Thomas Noble. Washington, D.C.: Catholic University of America Press, 1995.

Pope John Paul II. *Fides et Ratio.* Boston: Pauline, 1998.

———. *Veritatis Splendor.* Boston, MA: Pauline, 1993.

———. *The Redeemer of Man.* Boston, MA: Pauline Books, 1979.

———. *Man and Woman he Created Them: A Theology of the Body.* Translated by Michael Waldstein. Boston, MA: Pauline, 2006.

Ratzinger, Joseoph. *Introduction to Christianity.* Translasted by J. R. Foster. San Francisco: Ignatius, 1990.

René Descartes: Discourse on Method and Meditations on First Philosophy. Translated by Donald A. Cress. Fourth Edition. Indianapolis, IN: Hackett, 1998.

Rizzi, Anthony. *The Science Before Science: A Guide to Thinking in the 21st Century.* Baton Rouge, LA: Institute for Advanced Physics, 2004.

Schall, James V. *The Regensburg Lecture*. Chicago, IL: St. Augustine's, 2007.

Schönborn, Christoph. *Chance or Purpose: Creation, Evolution, and a Rational Faith*. Translated by Henry Taylor. San Francisco: Ignatius, 2007.

Spitzer, Robert J. *New Proofs for the Existence of God: Contributions of Contemporary Physics and Philosophy*. Grand Rapids, MI: Eerdmans, 2010.

Sri, Edward. *Men, Women, and the Mystery of Love: Practical Insights from John Paul II's Love and Responsibility*. Cincinnati, OH: Servant, 2007.

St. Thomas Aquinas. *Summa Theologica*. Translated by the Fathers of the English Dominican Province. New York: Benziger Bros, 1948.

Swafford, Andrew Dean. *Nature and Grace: A New Approach to Thomistic Ressourcement*. Eugene, OR: Pickwick, 2014.

———. "Finding the Way: My Journey from Football to Faith." *Kansas Monks* Spring 2014. Vol. 9. No. 1.

Vatican Council II: Constitutions Decrees Declarations. General. Editor, Austin Flannery. New York: Costello, 1996.

Veatch, Henry B. "The Problems and the Prospects of a Christian Philosophy— Then and Now." *The Monist* 75 (1992): 381–91.

Wojtyla, Karol. *Love and Responsibility*. Translated by H.T. Willets. San Francisco: Ignatius, 1993.

Woods, Thomas. *How the Catholic Church Built Western Civilization*. Washington, DC: Regenery, 2005.